A JOURNEY FROM ALEPPO TO JERUSAL[illegible]

AT EAS[illegible]

Note on Production

This book has been photographed from the original first edition. The quality of the type as reproduced on these pages therefore reflects the printing technology available at that time. A slight distortion of the type has also occurred during the photographic process, but this should not impair the reading of the text. We feel that the benefits outweigh the disadvantages of any minor distortions to the type.

THE FOLIOS ARCHIVE LIBRARY

A JOURNEY FROM ALEPPO TO JERUSALEM

AT EASTER, A.D. 1697

HENRY MAUNDRELL

FIRST PUBLISHED IN 1740 FOR
A. PEISLEY, BOOKSELLER IN OXFORD, AND
W. MEADOWS, BOOKSELLER IN CORNHILL, LONDON

Garnet
PUBLISHING

A Journey from Aleppo to Jerusalem
At Easter, A.D. 1697

Published by
Garnet Publishing Limited
8 Southern Court
South Street
Reading
RG1 4QS
UK
www.garnetpublishing.co.uk

New edition 2009
First published in 1740 for A. Peisley, Bookseller in Oxford, and W. Meadows, Bookseller in Cornhill, London

ISBN 978-1-85964-218-4

British Library Cataloguing-in-Publication Data
A catalogue record for this book is available from the British Library.

Jacket design by David Rose

A JOURNEY FROM *Aleppo* to *Jeruſalem* At Eaſter, *A. D.* 1697.

The Sixth Edition, To which is now added an Account of the Author's Journey to the Banks of Euphrates *at* Beer, *and to the Country of* Meſopotamia. *With an Index to the whole Work, not in any former Edition.*

By *Hen. Maundrell,* M. A. late Fellow of *Exeter* Coll. and Chaplain to the Factory at *Aleppo.*

OXFORD,
Printed at the THEATRE, for *A. Peiſley* Bookſeller in *Oxford,* and *W. Meadows* Bookſeller in *Cornhill, London.* MDCCXL.

Imprimatur,

GUIL. DELAUNE,

VICE-CAN. *OXON.*

April 8. 1703.

TO THE

READER.

THE Author of this ſhort Journal having ſometime ſince ſent a Copy of it into *England*, only for the private Entertainment of ſome of His Friends: They, finding with what a Spirit of Modeſty, Ingenuity and Truth it was written, ſoon reſolv'd to make it Publick. Upon notice hereof given to Him, He, with ſome unwillingneſs, ſubmitted to their Judgment as to the Publication; but withal deſired, that the Original might firſt be amended by the enſuing Corrections and Additions. He had made them partly from his own review of the Papers, after they had lain cold a good while by him; partly by the Advice of ſome Gentlemen of that Factory, who had ſince gone the ſame Journey, and had taken this Journal with them; and ſo gave it a new Authority by a freſh Examination of His Obſervations. But by misfortune his deſign'd Alterations did not arrive at *Oxford*, 'till the Book was almoſt printed off. Wherefore the Reader is deſired to accept candidly theſe following Emendations, which would have made the Work more perfect, if they could have been inſerted in the

Body of it, each in it's proper place. The Publishers thought a Piece ſo well writ, ought not to appear abroad without the uſual and proper Ornament of Writings of this kind, variety of Sculptures; and it having been deſign'd by the Author for a ſupplement to *Sandys*, their reſolution, at firſt, was to furniſh it with ſuch Cuts, as are wanting in Him; but *le Brune* being ſince publiſh'd, and in every ones hands, ſuch only are here inſerted, as are wanting in both.

☞ Note, *That the Corrections and Additions which were ſent by the Author after the Book was Printed off, are in this Edition inſerted in the Body of the Book in their proper places.*

TO THE

Right Reverend Father in GOD THOMAS Lord BISHOP of *ROCHESTER*.

MY LORD,

FROM a large and constant experience of your Lordships favour, I have all reason to believe that you will not think it tedious to hear something of my Affairs, tho' in themselves below your Lordships notice and regard.

It is now more than a twelve month since I arrived in this place; during all which time, I have had opportunity enough perfectly to observe and discover the Genius of the Factory, among whom my Lot is fallen. And upon the result of all my experience of them, I am obliged to give them this just Commendation; That they are a Society, highly meriting that excellent Character

racter which is given of them in England; *and which* (*besides the general vogue*) *your Lordship has sometime received from a most faithful and judicious hand, the excellent Bishop* Frampton. *As he undoubtedly was the great Improver of the rare temper of this Society, so he may well be esteemed best able to give them their true and deserved Character. I need only add, that such they still continue, as that incomparable Instructor left them: That is, Pious, Sober, Benevolent, devout in the Offices of Religion; in Conversation, innocently chearful; given to no pleasures but such as are honest and manly; to no Communications, but such as the nicest Ears need not be offended at; exhibiting in all their Actions those best and truest signs of a Christian Spirit, a sincere and chearful friendship among themselves, a generous Charity toward Others, and a profound reverence for the Liturgy and Constitution of the Church of* England. *It is our first Employment every morning to solemnize the dayly Service of the Church; at which I am sure to have always a devout, a regular and full Congregation. In a word, I can say no more (and less, I am sure, I ought not) than this, that in all my experience in the World, I have never known a Society of young Gentlemen, whether in the City, or Country,* (*I had almost said the University too*) *so well disposed in all points as this.*

Your Lordship will conclude, that in consequence of all this, my present Station cannot but be very agreeable. And tho' in leaving England, *I was separated from the greatest blessings to me in the World, your Lordships kindness, and that of my friends at* Richmond; *yet I must own, I have found here as much recompence, as could be made for such a separation.*

Among

Among other ſatisfactions, one great one, which I have had ſince my Arrival, was a Voyage to the Holy Land, in Company with fourteen others of our Factory. We went by way of the Coaſt; and having viſited the ſeveral places Conſecrated by the Life and Death of our Bleſſed Lord, we returned by way of Damaſcus. *If there be any thing either in theſe places which I have viſited, or elſewhere in theſe Countries, touching which, I may be capable of giving your Lordſhip any ſatisfaction, by my poor Obſervations, I ſhould eſteem it my great happineſs, and my coming thus far would ſeem compleatly recompenſed.*

I intreat your Lordſhips Bleſſing,

as being

Your Lordſhips

moſt dutiful,

humble Servant,

Hen. Maundrell.

TO MY

Ever Honoured Uncle

S[r] *CHARLES HEDGES* K[t],

Judge of the High Court

OF

ADMIRALTY of *ENGLAND*.

SIR,

I *AM ſenſible of two general Defects (and You will ſoon obſerve a great many more) running through this whole Paper, which might juſtly deter me from preſenting it to a Perſon of your great Learning and Judgment. One is, frequent Errours; the other, Tedioușneſs. But it is your pleaſure to require it from me as it is: and I am ſure whatever Faults there may be in it, yet there can be none ſo great, as it would be for me to diſpute your Injunctions. I have nothing to do therefore but to recommend it to your Favour, as it is offered up to your Commands, with all its Imperfections about it: only putting in a* word

word or two, before I dismiss it, by way of Apology.

And first, as to the Errours which you will be sure to note in it, I have this Mitigation to offer; that in a swift and transient View of places, (such as mine was) it was hardly possible for me, not to be sometimes overseen: But however this I profess with a clear Conscience, that whatever Mistakes there may be, yet there are no Lies.

As to the Tediousness of the Relations, the only Defence I have, is by sheltring my self in the Crowd: For it is a frailty more or less incident to most Men, especially Travellers, to abound, both in the sense they have, and in the Accounts they give, of their own Actions and Occurrences. If we light of any thing worth noting, We are apt to overflow in speaking of it; and too often We fall into that greater folly of recording such things for very considerable ones, as any disinterested Person would be ready to think, We could have no inducement to regard, but only because they relate to our own selves.

This is an Affectation, which however tastful it may be to the Persons who use it, yet (I know by my own Resentments of it) is to others most grating and disgustful.

When You come therefore to any such Nauseous places in this Journal, You may please to pass them over with that Contempt which they deserve, but nevertheless with some Indulgence to the Writer of them; for if this Vanity may be ever tolerated, Travellers are the Men who have the best Claim to that Favour. For it seems but a Reasonable Allowance, that they, who go through so many hazards and fatigues for the entertainment of others, should, in requital for all, be indulged a little in this sweet folly.

I might

I might in ſome meaſure, have remedied the fault I am now apologizing for, by reſcinding the dry part of the Journal; deſcribing Roads and diſtances, and Bearings of Places. But I conſidered, that this, tho' dry, was not without its uſe. And beſides, when I began to Obliterate, I ſoon found that if I ſhould go on, and ſtrike out all that I thought not worth writing to You, there would in the end be nothing but an univerſal Blot.

Be pleaſed therefore to accept the Whole as it was firſt ſet down, without Addition or Diminution; do with it as you pleaſe. When you are tired with reading it, You may ſupport your Patience as we did in Travelling it over, by conſidering, that what you are about is a Pilgrimage; that You need go it but once; and that 'tis the proper nature and deſign of ſuch performances, to have ſomething in them of Mortification.

Honoured Sir,

I am

Your moſt Dutiful Nephew,

and Obliged humble Servant,

Hen. Maundrell.

The Prospect of

ppo. Pag. 1

A JOURNEY FROM *Aleppo* to *Jerusalem* At Easter, *A. D.* 1697.

THERE being ſeveral Gentlemen of our Nation (four-teen in number) determined for a viſit to the *Holy-Land* at the approaching Eaſter, I reſolved, tho' but newly come to *Aleppo*, to make one in the ſame deſign: conſidering that as it was my purpoſe to undertake this Pilgrimage ſome time or other, before my Return to *England*, ſo I could never do it, either with leſs prejudice to my Cure, or with greater pleaſure to my ſelf than at this Juncture; having ſo large a part of my Congregation abroad at the ſame time, and in my Company.

Purſuant to this reſolution, we ſet out from *Aleppo* Friday *Feb.* 26. 1696. at three in the Afternoon, intending to make only a ſhort ſtep that Evening in order to prove how well we were provided with neceſſaries for our Journey. Our Quarters this firſt Night we took up at the *Honey-Kane*; a place of but indifferent Accommodation, about one hour and a half Weſt of *Aleppo*.

It muſt here be noted, that, in Travelling this Country, a Man does not meet with a Market-Town, and Inns, every night, as in *England*: The beſt reception you can find here, is either under your own Tent, if the ſeaſon permit; or elſe in certain publick Lodgments founded in Charity for the uſe of Travellers. Theſe are called by the Turks *Kanes*; and are ſeated ſometimes in the Towns and Villages; ſometimes at convenient diſtances upon the open Road. They are built in faſhion of a Cloiſter, encompaſſing a Court of thirty or forty Yards ſquare, more, or leſs, according to the meaſure of the Founder's Ability or Charity. At theſe places all Comers are free to take Shelter; paying only a ſmall Fee to the *Kane-keeper*, and very often without that acknowledgment. But muſt expect nothing here generally but bare walls: as for other Accommodations, of Meat, Drink, Bed, Fire, Provender; with theſe it muſt be every ones care to furniſh himſelf.

Saturday, Feb. 27.

From the *Honey-Kane* we parted very early the next Morning; and proceeding Weſterly as the day before, arrived in one hour and half at *Oo-rem*; an old Village affording nothing remarkable but the ruins of a ſmall Church. From *Oo-rem* we came in half an hour to *Keffre*; and in three quarters more to *Eſſoyn*. At this laſt place we enter'd into the plains of *Kefteen*: proceeding in which, we came in one hour to another Village called *Legene*, and half an hour more to *Hozano*, and in a good hour more to *Kefteen*. Our whole Stage this day was about five hours, our Courſe a little Southerly of the Weſt.

The Plains of *Kefteen* are of a vaſt Compaſs; extending to the Southward beyond the reach of the Eye, and in moſt places very fruitful and well cultivated. At our firſt deſcent into them at *Eſſoyn*, we counted twenty four Villages, or places at a diſtance reſembling Villages, within our View from one Station. The Soil is of a reddiſh colour, very looſe and hollow; and you ſee hardly a Stone in it. Whereas on its Weſt ſide there runs along for many Miles together a high ridge of Hills, diſcovering nothing but

but vaſt naked Rocks without the leaſt ſign of Mould, or any uſeful Production: which yields an appearance, as if Nature had, as it were, in kindneſs to the Husband-man, purged the whole plain of theſe Stones, and piled them all up together in that one Mountain. *Kefteen* it ſelf is a large plentiful Village on the Weſt ſide of the Plain. And the adjacent Fields abounding with Corn, give the Inhabitants great advantage for breeding Pidgeons: inſomuch that you find here more Dove-Cots than other Houſes. We ſaw at this place, over the door of a Bagnio a marble Stone, carved with the Sign of the ⊕ and the Δόξα Πατρὶ, &c. with a date not legible. It was probably the Portal of ſome Church in ancient times: for I was aſſured by the Inhabitants of the Village, that there are many Ruins of Churches and Convents ſtill to be ſeen in the Neighbouring rocky Mountains.

Sunday, Feb. 28.

Having a long Stage to go this day, we left *Kefteen* very early: And continuing ſtill in the ſame fruitful Plain abounding in Corn, Olives and Vines, we came in three quarters of an hour to *Harbanooſe*; a ſmall Village ſituated at the extremity of the Plain. Where, after croſſing a ſmall aſcent, we came into a very rich Valley called *Rooge*. It runs to the South farther than one can diſcern, but in breadth, from Eaſt to Weſt it extends not above an hours riding; and is walled in (as it were) on both ſides, with high rocky Mountains. Having travelled in this Valley near four hours, we came to a large Water called the Lake (or rather, according to the Oriental ſtyle, the Sea) of *Rooge*. Thro' the Skirt of this Lake we were obliged to paſs; and found it no ſmall trouble to get our Horſes, and much more our loaded Mules thro' the water and mire. But all the Sea was ſo dried up, and the road ſo perfectly amended at our return, that we could not then diſcern, ſo much as where the place was, which had given ſo great trouble. From this Lake, we arrived in one hour at *Te-ne-ree*; a place where we paid our first Caphar.

These Caphars are certain duties which Travellers are obliged to pay, at several passes upon the Road, to Officers, who attend in their appointed Stations to receive them. They were at first levied by Christians to yield a recompence to the Country for maintaining the ways in good repair, and scouring them from Arabs, and Robbers. The Turks keep up so gainful an usage still, pretending the same causes for it. But under that pretence they take occasion to exact from Passengers, especially Franks, arbitrary and unreasonable Sums; and instead of being a safeguard, prove the greatest Rogues and Robbers themselves.

At a large hour beyond this Caphar, our Road led us over the Mountains, on the West side of the Valley of *Rooge*. We were near an hour in crossing them, after which we descended into another Valley running parallel to the former, and parted from it only by the last ridge of Hills. At the first descent into this Valley is a Village called *Bell-Maez* from which we came in two hours to *Shoggle*. Our course was for the most part of this day, West-South-West. Our stage in all ten hours.

Shoggle is a pretty large, but exceeding filthy Town, situated on the River *Orontes*: over which you pass by a Bridge of thirteen small Arches to come at the Town. The River hereabouts is of a good breadth; and yet so rapid, that it turns great Wheels, made for lifting up the Water, by its natural swiftness, without any force added to it, by confining its Stream. It's Waters are turbid, and very unwholsome, and its Fish worse; as we found by experience, there being no Person of all our Company, that had eaten of them over night but found himself much indisposed the next Morning. We lodged here in a very large and handsome *Kane*, far exceeding what is usually seen in this sort of Buildings. It was founded by the second *Cuperli*, and endowed with a competent Revenue, for supplying every Traveller, that takes up his Quarters in it, with a competent portion of Bread, and

Broth,

Broth, and Flesh, which is always ready for those that demand it, as very few People of the Country fail to do. There is annext to the *Kane*, on its West side, another Quadrangle, containing apartments for a certain number of Alms-men; the charitable donation of the same *Cuperli*. The *Kane* we found at our arrival, crouded with a great number of Turkish Hadgees, or Pilgrims bound for *Meccha*. But neverthelesss we met with a peaceable Reception amongst them, tho' our Faces were set to a different place.

Monday Mar. 1.

From *Shoggle* our Road led us at first Westerly, in order to our crossing the Mountain on that side the Valley. We arrived at the foot of the ascent in half an hour, but met with such rugged and foul ways in the Mountains, that it took us up two hours to get clear of them. After which we descended into a third Valley, resembling the other Two which we had passed before. At the first entrance into it is a Village called *Be-da-me*, giving the same Name also to the Valley. Having travelled about two hours in this Valley, we entred into a Woody Mountainous Country, which ends the *Bashalick* of *Aleppo*, and begins that of *Tripoli*. Our Road here was very Rocky, and uneven; but yet the variety, which it afforded, made some amends for that inconvenience. Sometimes it led us under the cool shade of thick trees: sometimes thro' narrow Valleys, water'd with fresh murmuring Torrents: and then for a good while together upon the brink of a Precipice. And in all places it treated us with the prospect of Plants, and Flowers of divers kinds: as Myrtles, Oleanders, Cyclamens, Anemonies, Tulips, Marygolds, and several other sorts of Aromatick Herbs. Having spent about two hours in this manner we descended into a low Valley; at the bottom of which is a Fissure into the Earth, of a great depth; but withal so narrow that it is not discernible to the Eye till you arrive just upon it. Tho' to the Ear a notice of it is given at a great distance, by reason

reaſon of the Noiſe of a Stream running down into it from the Hills. We could not gueſs it to be leſs than thirty Yards deep. But it is ſo narrow that a ſmall Arch, not four Yards over, lands you on its other ſide. They call it *the Shecks Wife*: A Name given it from a Woman of that Quality, who fell into it, and, I need not add, periſhed. The depth of the Channel, and the noiſe of the Water, are ſo extraordinary, that one cannot paſs over it without ſomething of Horrour. The ſides of this Fiſſure are firm and ſolid Rock, perpendicular and ſmooth, only ſeeming to lie in a wavy form all down, as it were to comply with the motion of the Water. From which obſervation we were led to conjecture, that the Stream, by a long and perpetual current had, as it were, ſaw'n its own Channel down into this unuſual deepneſs: to which effect the Water's being penn'd up in ſo narrow a paſſage, and its hurling down Stones along with it by its rapidity, may have not a little contributed.

From hence, continuing our courſe thro' a Road reſembling that before deſcribed, we arrived in one hour at a ſmall even part of ground called *Hadyar ib Sultane*, or the Sultan's Stone. And here we took up our Quarters this Night under our Tents. Our Road this day pointed for the moſt part South Weſt, and the whole of our Stage was about ſeven hours and a half.

Tueſday, March 2.

We were glad to part very early this Morning from our Campagnia Lodging; the weather being yet too moiſt and cold for ſuch diſcipline. Continuing our Journey thro' Woods and Mountains, as the day before, we arrived in about one hour at the Caphar of *Cruſia*, which is demanded near a *Kane* of that Name; a *Kane* they call it, tho' it be in truth nothing elſe, but a cold comfortleſs Ruin on the top of a Hill by the way ſide.

From hence in about another hour we arrived at the foot of a Mountain called *Occaby*; or as the word denotes, difficult, and indeed we found its aſcent fully an-

ſwerable

The situation of Corus or Cyrus The Episcopal seat of Comagene. pag 7.

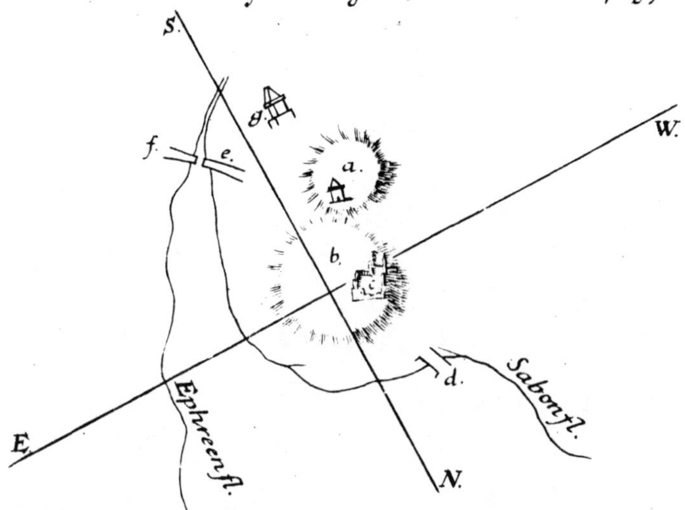

a. The Castle. b. The City. c. A Ruinous Fabrick. d. A Bridge probably one of those that were built by Theoderit. e.f. Two other Bridges of the same sort of Structure. g. A sepulchral Monument of a very antient and uncommon Structure

a. A mountain where formerly stood the Castle Acropolis.

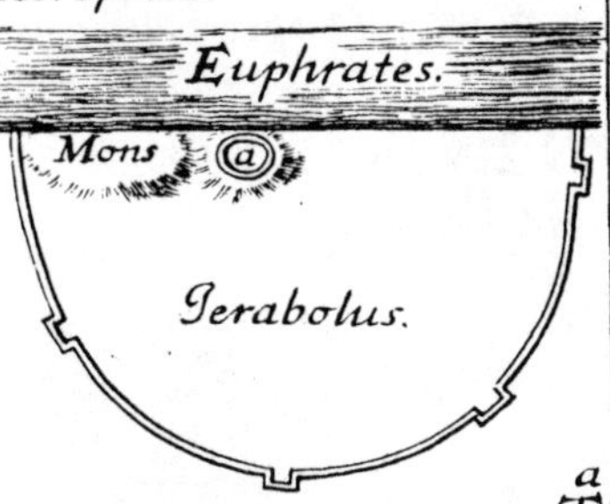

I found this figure Cut on a large stone at Ierabolus. The midle part was broken, and perhaps the Goddess Syra sat thereon but has been effaced by the Turks who are destroyers of Images for I have seen such a figure upon an Ancient coin of Hierapolis.

MB.

Three Inſcriptions over the Caſtle gate of Corus. pag. 7.

+ΒΙΛΛΙϹΑΡΙΟΥ ϹΤΡΑΤΕ
ΛΑΤΟΥΑΥΞΙΝΙΚΗ+

+ΙΟΥϹΤΙΝΙΑΝΟΥϹΤΟΥ
ΒΑϹΙΛΕΩϹ ΠΟΛΛ
ΤΑ ΕΤΗ ϯΟΕΥΔΩΡΑϹ
ΑΤΟΥϹΤΑϹΠΟΛΛ:
ΤΑ ΕΤΗ

+ΕΥϹΤΑΘΙΟΥ ΑΟ
Ν ΕϹΤΙΚΟΥΠΟΛΑΤΑ
ΕΤΗ ΑΤΩ ΘΕΟΥΧΑ

On a stone amongst yͤ. grave stones near yͤ. great Sepulcher at Corus.

D M
V · bP · VICTOR · I MM · LIINI
O LEG · VII · CL · EX · Z II · PR
POST · VIXIT · ANN · XXXVIII
MILITAVIT · ANN · XVI · AVR
MARTINVS · MIL · LEG · IIII
FL · FRATER · ET SECVNDVS
HERES · FRATRI · EXPR
O VINCIA · MOES · SVPER
REC ♡ VIMINAC
F · B · M · P ♡

Another in yͤ. Sameplace very imperfect.

AVR · VIND EX-
MILLE S VII CMX

A Bury. sculp.

ſwerable to its Name. The moiſture and ſlipperineſs of the way at this time, added to the ſteepneſs of it, greatly encreaſed our labour in aſcending it. Inſomuch that we were a full hour in gaining the top of the Hill. Here we found no more Woods or Hills, but a fine Country, well cultivated and planted with Silk Gardens: thro' which leaving on the right hand a Village called *Citte Galle*, inhabited ſolely by *Maronites*, we came in one hour to *Bellulca*. Here we repaired to a place which is both the *Kane* of the Village, and the *Aga's* Houſe; and reſolving by reaſon of the Rains, which fell very plentifully, to make this our Lodging, we went to viſit the *Aga* with a ſmall preſent in our hands, in order to procure our ſelves a civil Reception. But we found little recompence from his Turkiſh gratitude, for after all our reſpect to him, it was not without much importunity that we obtain'd to have the uſe of a dry part of the Houſe; The place where we were at firſt Lodged lying open to the Wind and the beating in of the Rain. Our whole Stage this day was not much above four hours, our courſe about South Weſt.

Being inform'd that here were ſeveral Chriſtian Inhabitants in this place, we went to viſit their Church, which we found ſo poor and pitiful a Structure, that here Chriſtianity ſeem'd to be brought to its humbleſt State, and Chriſt to be laid again in a Manger. It was only a Room of about four or five Yards ſquare, wall'd with Dirt, having nothing but the uneven ground for its Pavement; and for its Ceiling only ſome rude Traves laid athwart it, and cover'd with Buſhes to keep out the Weather. On the Eaſt ſide was an Altar, built of the ſame Materials with the Wall; only it was paved at top with Pot-ſherds and Slates, to give it the face of a Table. In the middle of the Altar ſtood a ſmall Croſs compos'd of two Laths nail'd together in the middle: on each ſide of which enſign were faſtned to the Wall two or three old Prints repreſenting our Bleſſed Lord and the Bleſſed Virgin, *&c.* The Venerable preſents of ſome Itinerant Fryars, that had

had paſſed this way. On the South ſide was a piece of plank ſupported by a Poſt, which we underſtood was the Reading Desk, juſt by Which, was a little hole commodiouſly broke thro' the Wall to give light to the Reader. A very mean habitation this for the God of Heaven! But yet held in great eſteem, and reverence by the poor People; who not only come with all Devotion hither themſelves, but alſo depoſite here whatever is moſt valuable to them, in order to derive upon it a Bleſſing. When we were there the whole Room was hang'd about with Bags of Silkworms Eggs; to the end that by remaining in ſo Holy a place, they might attract a Benediction, and a Virtue of encreaſing.

Wedneſday, Mar. 3.

The next Morning flatter'd us with the hopes of a fair day after the great Rains, which had fallen for near eight hours together. We therefore ventur'd to leave *Bellulca*, with no great thanks to it for our Entertainment. But we had not gone far, before we began to wiſh that we had kept our former Accommodation bad as it was; for the Rains began to break out afreſh with greater fury than before: nor had we more comfort under foot, the Road being very deep and full of ſloughs. However we reſolv'd to go forward in hopes of a better time, and in four hours (very long ones in ſuch uncomfortable Circumſtances) we arriv'd at *Sholfatia*, a poor Village ſituate upon a ſmall River which we were oblig'd to paſs. A River we might call it now, it being ſwollen ſo high by the late Rains, that it was impaſſable; tho' at other times it be but a ſmall Brook, and, in the Summer, perfectly dry.

Here inſtead of mending our Condition, as we expected, we began to drink more deeply of the bitter Cup of Pilgrims, being brought to ſuch a ſtrait, that we knew not which way to turn our ſelves. For (as I ſaid) the Stream was not fordable, ſo that there was no going forward; and as for facing about, and returning to the place from whence we came, that was a thing, we were very

very averſe to: Well knowing, by that Mornings experience, the badneſs of the Road; and likewiſe having reaſon to expect but a cold welcome at our Journeys end. As for Lodging in the Village, that was a thing not to be endured: For the Houſes were all fill'd with Dirt and Naſtineſs, being inhabited promiſcuouſly by the Villagers and their Cattle. As for lying in the Campagnia, the Rain was ſo vehement we could not do that, without an evident danger both to our Selves and Horſes.

But whilſt we were at this non-plus, not knowing which courſe to take, the Rain abated; and ſo we reſolved to pitch in the open Field, tho' thorowly ſoaked with the wet, eſteeming this however the leaſt evil. Accordingly we betook our Selves to a ſmall aſcent by the water's ſide, intending there, under our Tents, to wait the falling of the Stream.

We had not enjoy'd this ceſſation of Rain long, when it began to pour down afreſh, with terrible Lightning and Thunder. And now our Care was renewed, and we knew not well which to be moſt concern'd for; whether our Selves, who enjoyed the miſerable comfort of a dropping Tent over us, or for our Servants and Horſes which had nothing but their own Cloaths to protect them. At laſt there being a ſmall *Shecks* Houſe, or Burying-place hard by, we comforted our Selves with hopes that we might take Sanctuary there. The only difficulty was how to get admiſſion into ſo reverenc'd a place; the Turks being generally Men of greater Zeal than Mercy. To negotiate this affair we ſent a Turk (whom we had taken with us for ſuch occaſions) into the Village; ordering him to try firſt by fair means to gain admittance, and, if that fail'd, to threaten that we would enter by force. But the Religion of this place was of that kind which ſuperſedes inſtead of improving Humanity. The people abſolutely deny'd us the ſmall Charity we demanded; And ſent us word they would die upon our Swords before they would yield to have their Faith defil'd: Adding farther that it was their Faith to be true to *Hamet* and *Aly*, but

B to

to hate and renounce *Omar* and *Abu Beker*; and that this principle they were resolv'd to stand by. We told them we had as bad an opinion of *Omar* and *Abu Beker* as they could have: That we desir'd only a little shelter from the present Rain, and had no intention to defile their Faith. And thus with good words, we brought them to consent, that we might secure our Baggage in the *Shecks* House; but as for our Selves and Arms, 'twas our irreversible sentence to be excluded out of the hallow'd Walls. We were glad however to get the Merciless Doors open upon any terms; not doubting, but we should be able to make our advantage of it afterwards according to our desire: Which we actually did; for when it grew dark, and the Villagers were gone to sleep, we all got into the place of refuge, and there passed a Melancholy Night among the Tombs: Thus escaping however the greater evil of the Rain which fell all Night in great abundance.

Being now crept into the inside of the *Shecks* House, I must not omit, in requital for our Lodgings, to give some account of the nature of such Structures. They are stone Fabricks generally six or eight Yards square (more or less) and roofed with a Cupola, erected over the Graves of some eminent *Shecks*, that is, such Persons, as by their long Beards, Prayers of the same standard, and a kind of Pharisaical superciliousness (which are the great Virtues of the Mahometan Religion) have purchas'd to themselves the reputation of Learning and Saints.

Of these Buildings there are many scatter'd up and down the Country (for you will find among the Turks far more dead Saints than living ones.) They are situated commonly, tho' not always, upon the most eminent and conspicuous Ascents. To these Oratories the people repair with their Vows and Prayers, in their several distresses, much after the same manner, as the Romanists do to the shrines of their Saints. Only in this respect the practice of the Turks seems to be more Orthodox, in regard that tho' they make their Saint's shrine the House

of

of Prayer; yet they always make God alone, and not the Saint, the object of their addresses.

Thursday, *March* 4.

To revive us after the heaviness of the last Night, we had the consolation to be informed this Morning, that the River was fordable at a place a little farther down the Stream; and upon experiment we found it true as was reported. Glad of this discovery, we made the best dispatch we could to get clear of this inhospitable place; and according to our desires, soon arriv'd, with all our Baggage on the other side of the River.

From hence ascending gently for about half an hour, we came to the foot of a very steep Hill, which, when we had reached its top, presented us with the first prospect of the Ocean. We had in view likewise at about two hours distance to the Westward, the City *Latichea*, situate on a flat fruitful ground close by the Sea; A City first Built by *Seleucus Nicator*, and by him call'd in honour of his Mother Λαοδίκεια, which Name it retains with a very little corruption of it at this day. It was anciently a place of great Magnificence; but in the general Calamity which befel this Country, it was reduced to a very low condition, and so remain'd for a long time; But of late Years it has been encouraged to hold up its head again, and is rebuilt, and become one of the most flourishing places upon the Coast; being cherished, and put in a way of Trade by *Coplan Aga*, a Man of great wealth, and authority in these parts, and much addicted to Merchandise.

From the Hill which we last ascended, we had a small descent into a spacious Plain, along which we travelled Southward, keeping the Sea on the right hand, and a ridge of Mountains on the left. Having gone about one hour and a half in this Plain, we discern'd on the left hand, not far from the Road two ancient Tombs. They were Chests of Stone two Yards and a half long each. Their Cavities were cover'd over with large Tables of

Stone, that had been lifted aside probably in hopes of Treasure. The Chests were carved on the outside with Ox-heads, and wreaths hanging between them, after the manner of adorning Heathen Altars. They had likewise at first Inscriptions graven on them: But these were so eaten out, that One could not discover so much as the species of the Characters. Here were also several foundations of Buildings; but whether there were ever any place of Note situated hereabouts, or what it might be I cannot resolve.

Above an hour from these Tombs we came to another Stream which stopp'd our March again. These Mountain Rivers are ordinarily very inconsiderable: But they are apt to swell upon sudden Rains, to the destruction of many a Passenger, who will be so hardy as to venture unadvisedly over them. We took a more successful care at this place; for Marching about an hour higher up by the side of the Stream, we found a place, where the waters by dilating were become shallower, and there we got a safe passage to the other side. From hence we bent our Course to recover our former Road again; but we had not gone far, before there began a very violent Storm of Hail follow'd by a hard and continued Rain, which forced us to make the best of our way to *Jebilee*, leaving our Baggage to follow us at leisure.

Our whole Stage this day was about six hours, pointing for the first hour West, and for the remaining part near South, having the Sea on the right hand, and a ridge of Mountains at about two hours distance on the left. And in this state our Road continued for several days after, without any difference, save only that the Mountains at some places approach nearer the Sea; at other, retire farther off. These Mountains go under different Names in several places, as they run along upon the Coast, and are inhabited by rude People of several denominations. In that part of them above *Jebilee*, there dwell a people, called by the Turks *Neceres* of a very strange and singular Character. For 'tis their principle to adhere to no certain Religion; but Camelion-

like

like, they put on the Colour of Religion, whatever it be, which is reflected upon them from the Persons with whom they happen to converse. With Christians they profess themselves Christians; With Turks they are good Mussulmans; With Jews they pass for Jews; being such Proteus's in Religion, that no body was ever able to discover what shape or standard their Consciences are really of. All that is certain concerning them is, that they make very much and good Wine, and are great Drinkers.

Friday, Mar. 5.

This whole day we spent at *Jebilee* to recruit our Selves after our late fatigues; having the convenience of a new *Kane* to lodge in, Built at the North entrance into the City, by *Ostan* the present *Basha* of *Tripoli*.

Jebilee is seated close by the Sea, having a vast, and very fruitful Plain stretching round about it, on its other sides. It makes a very mean figure at present: Tho' it still retains the distinction of a City, and discovers evident footsteps of a better condition in former times. Its Ancient Name, from which also it derives its present, was *Gabala*; under which Name it occurs in *Strabo*, and other old Geographers. In the time of the Greek Emperours, it was dignify'd with a Bishop's See. In which sometimes sate *Severian* the Grand Adversary and Arch-Conspirator against St *Chrysostom*.

The most remarkable things, that appear here at this day, are a Mosque, and an Alms-house just by it, both Built by *Sultan Ibrahim*. In the former his Body is deposited, and we were admitted to see his Tomb, tho' held by the Turks in great Veneration. We found it only a great wooden Chest, erected over his Grave, and cover'd with a Carpet of painted Calico, extending on all sides down to the ground. It was also trick'd up with a great many long Ropes of wooden Beads hanging upon it, and somewhat resembling the furniture of a Button-maker's Shop. This is the Turks usual way of adorning the Tombs of their holy Men, as I have seen in several other instances.

instances. The long strings of Beads passing in this Country for marks of great Devotion and Gravity. In this Mosque we saw several large Incense Pots, Candlesticks for Altars, and other Church furniture, being the spoils of Christian Churches at the taking of *Cyprus*. Close by the Mosque is a very beautiful Bagnio, and a small Grove of Orange Trees; under the shade of which Travellers are wont to pitch their Tents in the Summer time.

The Turks, that were our conductors into the Mosque, entertain'd us with a long Story of this *Sultan Ibrahim* who lies there Interr'd; especially touching his mortification, and renouncing the World. They reported that having divested himself of his Royalty, he retir'd hither and liv'd twenty Years in a *Grotto* by the Sea side, dedicating himself wholly to Poverty and Devotion: And in order to confirm the truth of their relation, they pretended to carry us to the very *Cell* where he abode. Being come to the place, we found there a multitude of Sepulchres hewn into the Rocks by the Sea side, according to the Ancient manner of Burying in this Country: And amongst these they shew'd one, which they averr'd to be the very place in which the devout *Sultan* exercised his twenty Years discipline; and to add a little probability to the Story, they shew'd, at a small distance, another Grotto twice as large as any of its fellows, and uncover'd at the top, which had three Niches or Praying places hewn in its South side. This they would have to be *Sultan Ibrahim*'s Oratory: It being the manner of the Turks always to make such Niches in their Mosques and other places of Devotion, to denote the Southern quarter of the World; for that way the Mussulmans are obliged to set their faces when they Pray, in reverence to the Tomb of their Prophet. These Niches are always form'd exactly resembling those usually made for Statues, both in their size, fabrick, and every circumstance. I have sometimes reflected for what reason the Turks should appoint such Marks to direct their faces toward in Prayer. And if I may be allow'd to conjecture, I believe they did

did it at first in testimony of their Iconoclastick principle; and to express to them both the reality of the Divine presence there, and at the same time also its Invisibility. The Relators of this Story of *Sultan Ibrahim* were doubtless fully persuaded of the truth of it themselves. But we could not tell what conjectures to make of it, having never met with any account of such a *Sultan*, but only from this rude Tradition.

From these Mahometan Sanctuaries, our Guide pretended to carry us to a Christian Church, about two furlongs out of Town on the South side. When we came to it, we found it nothing but a small Grotto in a Rock, by the Sea shore, open on the side towards the Sea; and having a rude pile of Stones erected in it for an Altar. In our return from this poor Chappel, we met with the Person who was the Curate of it. He told us that Himself and some few other Christians of the Greek Communion, were wont to assemble in this humble *Cell* for Divine Service, being not permitted to have any place of Worship within the Town.

Jebilee seems to have had Anciently some convenience for Shipping. There is still to be seen a ridge compos'd of huge square Stones running a little way into the Sea; which appears to have been formerly continued farther on, and to have made a Mole. Near this place we saw a great many Pillars of Granite, some by the Water side, others tumbled into the Water. There were others in a Garden close by, together with Capitals of white Marble finely carv'd; which testify in some measure the Ancient Splendor of this City.

But the most considerable Antiquity in *Jebilee*, and greatest Monument of its former Eminency, is the remains of a Noble Theater just at the North Gate of the City. It passes amongst the Turks for an old Castle; which (according to the Asiatick way of enlarging) they report to have been of so prodigious a height, when in its perfect state, that a Horseman might have rid, about Sun-rising, a full hour in the shade of it.

As

As for what remains of this mighty *Babel*, it is no more than twenty Foot high. The flat side of it has been blown up with Gun-powder by the Turks. And from hence (as they related) was taken a great quantity of Marble, which we saw used in adorning their Bagnio and Mosque before mention'd. All of it that is now standing is the Semi-Circle. It extends from corner to corner just a hundred Yards. In this Semi-Circular part is a range of seventeen round Windows just above the ground, and between the Windows all round were raised, on high Pedestals, large Massey Pillars, standing as Buttresses against the Wall, both for the strength and ornament of the Fabrick; but these supporters are at present most of them broken down.

Within is a very large Arena, but the just measure of it could not be taken, by reason of the Houses with which the Turks have almost fill'd it up. On the West side the seats of the Spectators remain still entire, as do likewise the Caves or Vaults which run under the Subsellia all round the Theatre. The outward Wall is three Yards three quarters thick, and built of very large and firm Stones; which great strength has preserv'd it thus long from the Jaws of time, and from that general ruin, which the Turks bring with them into most places where they come.

Saturday, Mar. 6.

Having done with *Jebilee*, we put forward again early the next Morning, with a prospect of much better weather than we had been attended with, in our former motions. Our Road continued by the Sea side, and in about two hours, brought us to a fair deep River, called by the Turks *Naher-il-Melech*, or the King's River. Here we saw some heaps of ruins on both sides of the River, with several Pillars of Granite, and other footsteps of some considerable Buildings. About half an hour farther we passed another River called *Jobar*, shewing the remains of a Stone-bridge over it, once well Built but

now

now broken down. On the other ſide of this River in a large plough'd Field, ſtood a great ſquare Tower; and round about, the rubbiſh of many other Buildings. Likewiſe all along this day's Journey, we obſerv'd many Ruins of Caſtles and Houſes, which teſtify that this Country, however it be neglected at preſent, was once in the hands of a people that knew how to value it, and thought it worth the defending. *Strabo* calls this whole Region from *Jebilee* as far as *Aradus*, the Country of the *Aradii* (of whom in due place) and gives us the Names of ſeveral places ſituate anciently along this Coaſt; As *Paltus*, *Balanea*, *Caranus*, *Enydra*, *Marathus*, *Ximyra*. But whether the Ruins which we ſaw this day, may be the remains of any of thoſe Cities, cannot well be determin'd at this diſtance of time; ſeeing all we have of thoſe places, is only their names, without any ſufficient diſtinctions, by which to diſcover their Situation. The *Balanea* of *Strabo* is indeed ſaid to be ſtill extant, being ſuppos'd to be the ſame place, that the Turks (little changing its Name) call at this day *Baneas*. This place is four good hours beyond *Jebilee*. It ſtands upon a ſmall declivity about a furlong diſtant from the Sea, and has a fine clear Stream running ſwiftly by it on the South ſide. It is at preſent uninhabited, but its Situation proves it to have been anciently a pleaſant, its Ruins a well-built, and its Bay before it, an advantagious Habitation. At this place was required another Caphar.

Leaving *Baneas*, we went on by the Sea ſide, and in about a quarter of an hour paſſed by an old Caſtle, on the top of a very high Mountain. It is built in the figure of an Equilateral Triangle, having one of its Angles pointing towards the Sea. The Turks call it *Merchab*; and enlarge much upon the Sieges it has ſuſtain'd in former times: But whatever force it may have had anciently, it is at preſent only a reſidence for poor Country people. This is probably the ſame Caſtle mention'd by *Adrichomius* and others under the Name of *Margath*; to which the Biſhops of *Balanea* were forced to tranſlate their *See* by reaſon of the inſults of the *Saracens.*

At about one hour and a half diſtance from *Baneas*, we came to a ſmall clear Stream, which induced us to take up our Lodging near it. We pitch'd in the Campagnia about two or three furlongs up from the Sea; having in ſight on the Mountains above us, a Village called *Sophia*, inhabited ſolely by Maronites; and a little farther *Beſack*, another Village poſſeſs'd by Turks only; and a little farther *Merakiah*, whoſe Inhabitants are a Miſcellany of Chriſtians and Turks together. Our whole Stage this day was about ſix hours.

Sunday, Mar. 7.

From this Quarter we remov'd early the next Morning, and in three hours came to a fair deep River called *Nahor Huſſine*; having an old Bridge turn'd over it, conſiſting of only one Arch, but that very large and exceeding well wrought. In one hour and a half more, travelling ſtill by the Sea ſide, we reach'd *Tortoſa.*

The ancient Name of this place was *Orthoſia*. It was a Biſhop's See in the Province of *Tyre*. The Writers of the holy Wars make frequent mention of it, as a place of great ſtrength. And one may venture to believe them, from what appears of it at this day.

Its ſituation is on the Sea-ſhore; having a ſpacious Plain extending round about it on its other ſides. What remains of it is the Caſtle, which is very large and ſtill inhabited. On one ſide, it is waſh'd by the Sea; On the others, it is fortified by a double Wall of courſe Marble, Built after the Ruſtick manner. Between the two Walls is a Ditch; as likewiſe is another encompaſſing the outermoſt Wall. You enter this Fortreſs on the North ſide, over an old Draw-bridge, which lands you in a ſpacious Room now for the moſt part uncover'd, but anciently well arch'd over, being the Church belonging to the Caſtle. On one ſide it reſembles a Church, and in witneſs of its being ſuch, ſhews at this day, ſeveral holy Emblems carv'd upon its Walls, as that of a Dove deſcending, over the

the place where ſtood the Altar; and in another place that of the Holy-Lamb. But on the ſide which fronts outward, it has the face of a Caſtle, being built with Port-holes for Artillery, inſtead of Windows. Round the Caſtle on the South and Eaſt ſides ſtood anciently the City. It had a good Wall and Ditch encompaſſing it, of which there are ſtill to be ſeen conſiderable remains. But for other Buildings, there is nothing now left in it, except a Church, which ſtands about a furlong Eaſtward from the Caſtle. It is one hundred and thirty foot in length, in breadth ninety three, and in height ſixty one. Its Walls, and Arches, and Pillars, are of a Baſtard Marble, and all ſtill ſo entire, that a ſmall expence would ſuffice to recover it into the ſtate of a beautiful Church again. But, to the grief of any Chriſtian Beholder, it is now made a ſtall for Cattle, and we were, when we went to ſee it, almoſt up to our knees in Dirt and Mire.

From *Tortoſa* we ſent our baggage before us, with orders to advance a few Miles farther toward *Tripoli*, to the intent that we might ſhorten our Stage to that place the next day. We follow'd not long after, and in about a quarter of an hour came to a River, or rather a Channel of a River, for it was now almoſt dry: Tho' queſtionleſs here muſt have been anciently no inconſiderable Stream; as we might infer both from the largeneſs of the Channel, and the fragments of a Stone-bridge, formerly laid over it.

In about half an hour more, we came a Breſt with a ſmall Iſland, about a League diſtant from the ſhore, called by the Turks *Ru-ad*. This is ſuppoſed to be the ancient *Arvad*, *Arphad*, or *Arpad*, (under which ſeveral names it occurs, 2 *Kin*. 19. 13. *Gen*. 10. 18. *Ezek*. 27. 11. &c) and the *Aradus* of the Greeks and Romans. It ſeemed to the Eye to be not above two or three furlongs long; and was wholly filled up with tall Buildings like Caſtles. The ancient Inhabitants of this Iſland were famous for Navigation, and had a command upon the Continent as far as *Gabala*.

About a quarter of an hour farther we came up with our Muliteers; they having pitched our Tents, before they had gone ſo far as we intended. But this Miſcarriage they well recompenſed, by the condition of the place where they ſtopp'd; it affording us the Entertainment of ſeveral notable Antiquities, which we might otherwiſe perhaps have paſs'd by unobſerv'd. It was at a green Plat lying within one hour of *Tortoſa*, a little Southward of *Aradus*, and about a quarter of a mile from the Sea, having in it a good Fountain (tho' of a bad name) called the *Serpent Fountain*.

The firſt Antiquity that we here obſerved was a large Dike thirty yards over at top, cut into the firm Rock. Its ſides went ſloping down with Stairs form'd out of the natural Rock, deſcending gradually from the top to the bottom. This Dike ſtretch'd in a direct line, Eaſt and Weſt more than a furlong, bearing ſtill the ſame figure of Stairs running in right lines all along its ſides. It broke off at laſt at a flat marſhy ground, extending about two furlongs betwixt it and the Sea. It is hard to imagine that the Water ever flow'd up thus high; and harder, (without ſuppoſing that) to reſolve, for what reaſon all this pains of cutting the Rock in ſuch a faſhion, was taken.

This Dike was on the North ſide of the *Serpent Fountain*; and juſt on the other ſide of it, we eſpy'd another Antiquity, which took up our next obſervation. There was a Court of fifty five yards ſquare, cut in the natural Rock; the ſides of the Rock ſtanding round it, about three yards high, ſupplied the place of Walls. On three ſides it was thus encompaſſed; but to the Northward it lay open. In the Center of this Area was a ſquare part of the Rock left ſtanding; being three yards high and five yards and a half ſquare. This ſerv'd for a Pedeſtal to a Throne erected upon it. The Throne was compos'd of four large Stones, two at the Sides, one at the Back, another hanging over all at Top, in the manner of a Canopy. The whole Structure was about twenty foot high, fronting toward that ſide where the Court was open. The Stone that

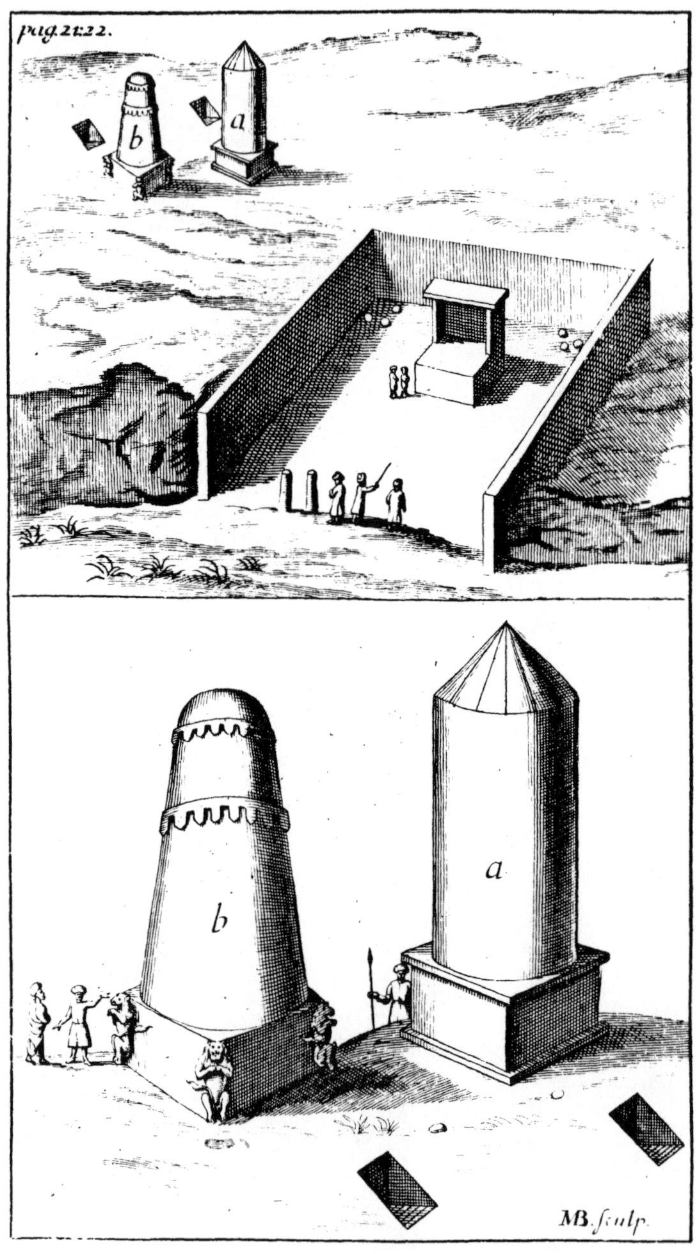
pag.21.22.
b
a
b
a
MB. sculp.

that made the Canopy was five yards and three quarters ſquare, and carv'd round with a handſome Corniſh. What all this might be deſign'd for, we could not imagine; unleſs perhaps the Court may paſs for an Idol-Temple, and the Pile in the middle for the Throne of the Idol: Which ſeems the more probable, in regard that *Hercules*, i. e. the Sun, the great abomination of the Phenicians, was wont to be adored in an open Temple. At the two innermoſt Angles of the Court, and likewiſe on the open ſide were left Pillars of the natural Rock; three at each of the former and two at the latter.

About half a mile to the Southward of the foreſaid Antiquities there ſtood in view two Towers. But it growing dark, we were forced to defer our examination of them till the next Morning. Our whole Stage this day exceeded not ſix hours.

Monday, March 8.

Having paſſed over a reſtleſs night, in a marſhy and unwholſome ground, we got up very early; in order to take a nearer view of the two Towers laſt mention'd. We found them to be Sepulchral Monuments, erected over two ancient Burying places. They ſtood at about ten yards diſtance from each other, and their ſhape and fabrick is repreſented in the figures (a) and (b).

The Tower (a) was thirty three foot high. Its longeſt Stone or Pedeſtal was ten foot high, and fifteen ſquare: The ſuperſtructure upon Which, was firſt a tall Stone in form of a Cylinder; and then another Stone cut in ſhape of a Pyramid.

The other Tower (b) was thirty foot and two inches high. Its Pedeſtal was in height ſix foot; and ſixteen foot ſix inches ſquare. It was ſupported by four Lyons carv'd one at each corner of the Pedeſtal. The Carving had been very rude at beſt; but was now rendred by time much worſe. The upper part rear'd upon the Pedeſtal was all one ſingle ſtone, in faſhion as is repreſented in the figure (b).

Each

Each of these barbarous Monuments had under it several Sepulchers; the Entrances into which, were on the South side. It cost us some time and pains to get into them; the Avenues being obstructed, first with Briars and Weeds, and then with Dirt. But however we remov'd both these Obstacles; encouraging our selves with the Hopes, or rather making our selves merry with the Fancy of hidden Treasure. But as soon as we were enter'd into the Vaults, we found that our golden Imaginations ended (as all worldly hopes and projects do at last) in Dust, and Putrefaction. But however that we might not go away without some reward for our pains, we took as exact a survey as we could of these Chambers of darkness; which were dispos'd in such manner as is express'd in the following Figures.

The Chambers under the Tower (a) lay as is represented in the first Figure. Going down seven or eight steps, you come to the mouth of the Sepulcher; where crawling in you arrive in the Chamber (1) which is nine foot two inches broad and eleven foot long. Turning to the right hand, and going thro' a narrow Passage you come to the Room (2) which is eight foot broad and ten long. In this Chamber are seven Cells for Corpses, *viz.* two over against the entrance, four on the left hand and one unfinish'd on the right. These Cells were hewn directly into the firm Rock. We measur'd several of them, and found them eight foot and a half in length, and three foot three inches square. I would not infer from hence that the Corpses deposited here, were of such a Gigantick size, as to fill up such large Coffins: Tho' at the same time, why should any Men be so prodigal of their labour, as to cut these Caverns into so hard a Rock as this was, much farther than Necessity requir'd?

On the other side of the Chamber (1) was a narrow passage seven foot long leading into the Room (3) whose Dimensions were nine foot in breadth and twelve in length. It had eleven Cells of somewhat a less size than the former lying at equal distances all round about it.

Passing

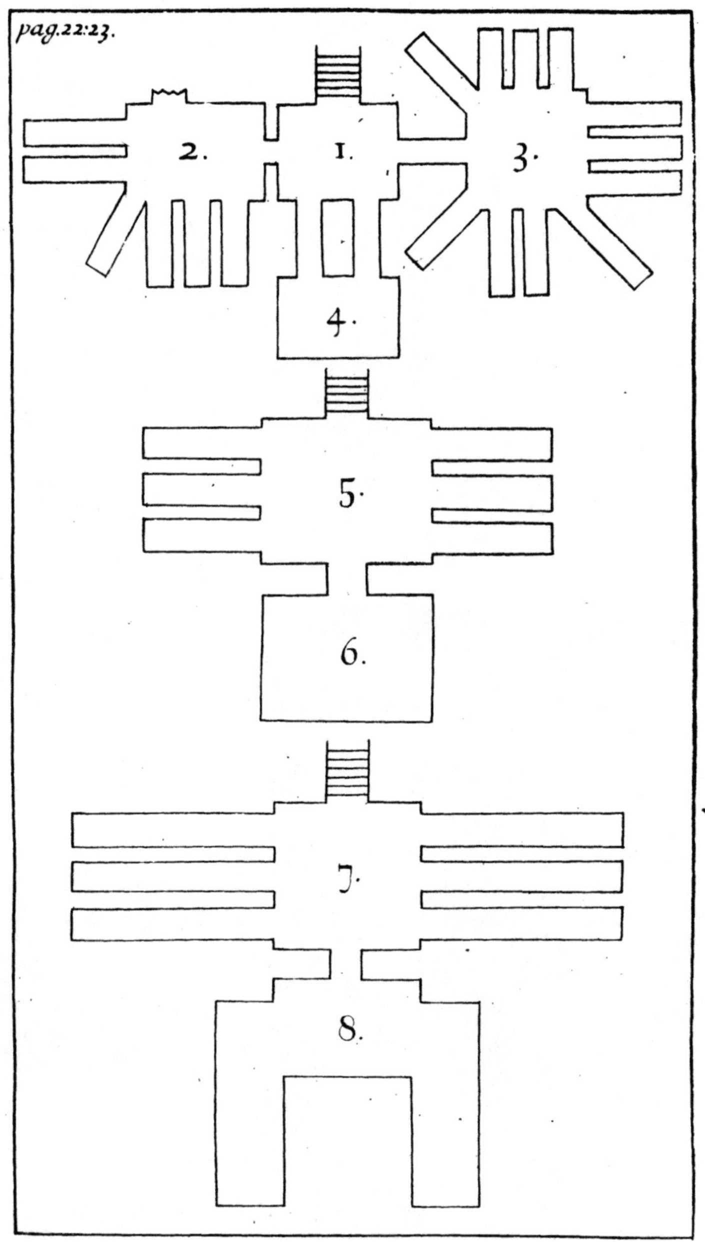
pag.22:23.
1.
2.
3.
4.
5.
6.
7.
8.

Passing out of the Room (1) foreright you have two narrow entrances, each seven foot long, into the Room (4). This Apartment was nine foot square: It had no Cells in it like the others; Nor any thing else remarkable, but only a Bench, cut all along its side on the left hand. From the Description of this Sepulcher, it is easy to conceive the Disposition of the other; which is represented in the figure (5. 6). The height of the Rooms in Both, was about six foot; and the Towers were built each over the innermost Room of the Sepulchers, to which it belonged.

At about the distance of a furlong from this place, we discern'd another Tower, resembling this last describ'd. It was erected likewise over a Sepulcher, of which you have the Delineation in the figure (7) and (8). There was this Singularity observable in this last Sepulcher; that its Cells were cut into the Rock eighteen foot in length, possibly to the intent, that two or three Corpses might be deposited in each of them, at the feet of one another. But having a long Stage this day to *Tripoli*, we thought it not seasonable to spend any more time in this place; which might perhaps have afforded us several other Antiquities.

And yet for all our haste, we had not gone a Mile, before our Curiosity was again arrested by the Observation of another Tower, which appear'd in a Thicket not far from the way side. It was thirty three foot and a half high, and thirty one foot square; compos'd of huge square Stones, and adorn'd with a handsome Cornish all round at Top. It contain'd only two Rooms one above the other; Into Both which, there were Entrances on the North-side thro' two square holes in the Wall. The Separation between Both Rooms, as also the Covering at the top, was made, not of Arch'd-work, but of vast flat Stones; in thickness four foot, and so great an Extent, that two of them in each place, sufficed to spread over the whole Fabrick. This was a very ancient Structure, and probably a place of Sepulture.

I must

I must not forget, that round about the *Serpent Fountain*, and also as far as this last Tower, we saw many Sepulchers, old Foundations, and other remains of Antiquity. From all which it may be assuredly concluded, that here must needs have been some famous Habitation in ancient Times: But whether this might be the *Ximyra*, laid down by *Strabo* hereabouts (or as *Pliny* calls it,, *Lib.* 5. *Nat. Hist. Cap.* 20. *Simyra)* the same possibly with the Country of the *Zemarites*, mention'd in conjunction with the *Arvadites*, *Gen.* 10. 18. I leave to others to discuss.

Having quitted our selves of these Antiquities, we enter'd into a spacious Plain, extending to a vast breadth, between the Sea and the Mountains; and in length reaching almost as far as *Tripoli*. The People of the Country call it *Junia*, that is, the Plain; which name they give it by way of Eminency, upon account of its vast Extent. We were full seven hours in passing it; and found it all along exceeding fruitful, by reason of the many Rivers and the great plenty of Water, which it enjoys. Of these Rivers the first is about six hours before you come to *Tripoli*. It has a Stone-Bridge over it, of three large Arches; and is the biggest Stream in the whole Plain: For which reason it goes by the name of *Nahor il Kibber*, or the great River. About half an hour farther you come to another River, called *Nahor Abrosh*, or the Leper's River. In three quarters of an hour more you pass a third River, called *Nahor Acchar*; having a handsome Stone-Bridge, of one very large Arch, laid over it. Two good hours more brings you to a fourth River, called ——— or the *cold Waters*, with a Bridge of three Arches over it. From hence you have two good hours more to *Tripoli*. I took the more exact account of all these Streams to the intent that I might give some light, for the better deciding that difference, which is found in Geographers, about the place of the River *Eleutherus*. The Moderns, all with one consent, give that name to a River between *Tyre* and *Sidon*, called by the Turks *Casimeer*. But this contradicts the universal Testimony of the Ancients, who place *Eleu-*

Eleutherus more Northward. *Strabo* will have it somewhere between *Orthosia* and *Tripoli*, as a Boundary dividing *Syria* from *Phœnicia* (p. 518,) *Pliny* places it near *Orthosia*, emptying it self into the Sea over against *Aradus*, *Nat. Hist. Lib.* 5. *C.* 20. The Writer of the *Maccabees* 1 *Macc.* 12. 25. 30. lays it in the Land of *Hamath*; which Country, whatever it were, was certainly without the Borders of *Israel*, as appears from the same Author. To this *Josephus* agrees, placing *Eleutherus* to the North of *Sidon*, as may be collected from him, *Lib.* 14. *Antiq. Jud. Cap.* 7. 8. where, speaking of *Mark Anthony*'s Donation to *Cleopatra*, he reports, how that Extravagant Gallant gave her all the Cities between *Eleutherus* and *Egypt*, except *Tyre* and *Sidon*. *Ptolemy* as cited by *Terranius*, places it yet more Northerly, between *Orthosia* and *Balanea*. From all which it is evident, that this cannot be the true ancient *Eleutherus* which the Moderns assign for it. But that Name is rather to be ascrib'd to one of these Rivers, crossing the Plain of *Junia*: Or else (if *Pliny's* Authority may be rely'd upon) to that River (now dry) which I mention'd a little on this side of *Tortosa*, and which has it's Mouth almost opposite to *Aradus*. But I will not determine any thing in this point, contenting my self to have given an account of the several Rivers as we pass'd them.

Tuesday, Mar. 9.

Drawing towards *Tripoli*, our Muletiers were afraid to advance, lest their Beasts might be press'd for publick service; as they were afterwards, in spight of all their Caution, to our great Vexation. So we left them in the Plain of *Junia*, and proceeded our selves for *Tripoli*; where we arriv'd about Sun-set. Our whole Stage this day was ten hours.

At *Tripoli* we repos'd a full Week, being very generously entertain'd by Mr *Francis Hastings* the Consul, and Mr *John Fisher* Merchant; theirs being the only English House in *Tripoli*.

D *Tripoli*

Tripoli is seated about half an hour from the Sea. The major part of the City lies between two Hills; one on the East, on which is a Castle commanding the place; another on the West, between the City and the Sea. This latter is said to have been at first rais'd and to be still encreas'd by the dayly accession of Sand, blown to it from the Shore: Upon which occasion there goes a Prophecy, that the whole City shall in time be buried with this Sandy Hill. But the Turks seem not very apprehensive of this Prediction; for instead of preventing the growth of the Hill, they suffer it to take its Course, and make it a place of Pleasure, which they would have little inclination to do, did they apprehend it were sometime to be their Grave.

Wednesday, March 10.

This day we were all treated by Mr *Fisher* in the Campagnia. The place where we dined was a narrow pleasant Valley by a River's side, distant from the City about a Mile Eastward. A-cross the Valley there runs from Hill to Hill a handsome lofty Aqueduct, carrying upon it so large a body of Water, as suffices the whole City. It was called the *Princes-bridge*, suppos'd to have been Built by *Godfrey* of *Bulloign*.

Thursday, Mar. 11.

This day we all dined at Consul *Hastings*'s House, and after dinner went to wait upon *Ostan* the *Bassa* of *Tripoli*, having first sent our Present, as the manner is amongst the Turks, to procure a propitious reception.

It is counted uncivil to visit in this Country without an Offering in hand. All great Men expect it as a kind of Tribute due to their Character and Authority; and look upon themselves as affronted, and indeed defrauded, when this Compliment is omitted. Even in familiar Visits amongst inferiour People, you shall seldom have them come without bringing a Flower, or an Orange, or some other such token of their respect to the Person visited: The Turks in this point keeping up the ancient Oriental Custom

hinted,

hinted, 1 *Sam.* 9. 7. *If we go* (says Saul) *what shall we bring the man of God? there is not a present*, &c. which words are questionless to be understood in conformity to this Eastern Custom, as relating to a token of Respect, and not to a price of Divination.

Friday, Mar. 12.

In the Afternoon we went to visit *Bell-Mount* a Convent of Greeks, about two hours to the Southward of *Tripoli*. It was founded by one of the Earls of *Tripoli*, and stands upon a very high Rocky Mountain, looking over the Sea; a place of very difficult Ascent, tho' made as accessible as it was capable by the labour of the poor Monks. It was our fortune to arrive there just as they were going to their Evening Service. Their Chappel is large but obscure; and the Altar is inclos'd with Cancelli, so as not to be approach'd by any one but the Priest, according to the fashion of the Greek Churches. They call their Congregation together, by beating a kind of a Tune with two Mallets on a long pendulous piece of plank at the Church door; Bells being an abomination to the Turks.

Their service consisted in precipitate, and very irreverent chattering of certain Prayers and Hymns to our blessed Saviour, and to the blessed Virgin, and in some dark Ceremonies; the Priest that officiated spent at least one third part of his time, in compassing the Altar, and perfuming it with a pot of Incense, and then going all round the Congregation flinging his Incense-pot backward and forward, and tendring its smoak with three repeated Vibrations to every Person present. Towards the end of the Service, there was brought into the Body of the Church, a small Table, cover'd with a fair linnen Cloth, on which were placed five small Cakes of Bread cross way in this form ⁘, and in the Center of each Cake was fix'd a small lighted wax Taper, a hole in the Cake serving for a Socket.

At this Ceremony, the Prieſt read the Goſpel concerning our Lord's feeding the Multitude with five Loaves. After which, the Bread was carried into the Cancelli, and being there ſuddenly broke to Bits, was again brought out in a Basket, and preſented to every one in the Aſſembly, that he might take a little. After this Collation, the Prieſt pronounc'd the Bleſſing, and ſo the Service ended. On both ſides of the Body of the Church, were ſeats for the Monks, in the nature of the Stalls for the Fellows of Colleges in *Oxford*; and on each hand of every Seat were placed Crutches. Theſe you find in like manner in moſt Churches of this Country. Their uſe is for the Prieſt to lean upon: The Service being ſometimes ſo long, that they cannot well ſtay it out, without the aſſiſtance of ſuch Eaſements; for they are not permitted by their Rubrick to ſit down. The younger Monks, who perhaps may have no great occaſion for theſe Supporters, do yet delight to uſe them (as the *Spaniards* do Spectacles) not for any Neceſſity, but in affectation of Gravity.

The Monks of this Convent were, as I remember, Forty in all. We found them ſeemingly a very good natur'd, and induſtrious, but certainly, a very ignorant People. For I found upon enquiry, they could not give any manner of Rationale of their own Divine Service. And to ſhew their extream ſimplicity, I cannot omit a Complement made to the Conſul by the chief of them, *viz.* that he was as glad to ſee him, as if he had beheld the *Meſſiah* himſelf coming in perſon to make a viſit to him.

Nor is this Ignorance to be much wondered at; for what Intervals of time they have between their hours of Devotion, they are forced to ſpend, not in Study, but in managing of their Flocks, cultivating their Land, pruning their Vineyards, and other labours of Husbandry, which they accompliſh with their own hands. This toyl they are obliged to undergo, not only to provide for their own ſuſtenance, but alſo that they may be able to ſatisfy the unreaſonable Exactions, which the greedy Turks, upon every pretence they can invent, are ready to impoſe upon them.

them. But that it may be the better gueſs'd what ſort of Men theſe Greek Monks are, I will add this farther Indication, *viz.* that the ſame Perſon, whom we ſaw officiating at the Altar, in his embroyder'd Sacerdotal Robe, brought us the next day, on his own back, a Kid, and a Goat's Skin of Wine, as a Preſent from the Convent.

Saturday, Mar. 13.

This Morning we went again to wait upon *Oſtan Baſſa* by his own appointment; and were entertain'd as before with great Courteſy. For you muſt know that the Turks are not ſo ignorant of Civility, and the Arts of endearment, but that they can practiſe them with as much Exactneſs, as any other Nation, whenever they have a mind to ſhew themſelves obliging. For the better apprehending of which, it may not be improper, nor unpleaſant here to deſcribe the Ceremonies of a Turkiſh viſit, as far as they have ever fallen under my obſervation, either upon this or any other occaſions.

When you would make a viſit to a Perſon of Quality here, you muſt ſend one before with a Preſent to beſpeak your admiſſion, and to know at what hour your coming may be moſt ſeaſonable. Being come to the Houſe, the Servants receive you at the outermoſt Gate, and conduct you toward their Lord or Maſter's Apartment; other Servants (I ſuppoſe of better Rank) meeting you in the way, at their ſeveral Stations, as you draw nearer to the Perſon you viſit. Coming into his Room, you find him prepar'd to receive you, either ſtanding at the edge of the Duan, or elſe lying down at one corner of it, according as he thinks it proper to maintain a greater or leſs Diſtinction. Theſe Duans are a ſort of low Stages, ſeated in the pleaſanteſt part of the Room, elevated about ſixteen or eighteen inches or more above the Floor. They are ſpread with Carpets, and furniſhed all round with Bolſters for leaning upon. Upon theſe the Turks eat, ſleep, ſmoak, receive viſits, ſay their prayers, *&c.* Their whole delight

is

is in lolling upon them, and in furniſhing them richly out is their greateſt Luxury.

Being come to the ſide of the Duan, you ſlip off your Shoes, and ſtepping up take your place; which you muſt do firſt at ſome diſtance, and upon your knees, laying your hands very formally before you. Thus you muſt remain, till the Man of Quality invites you to draw nearer, and to put your ſelf in an eaſier poſture, leaning upon the Bolſter. Being thus fix'd, he diſcourſes with you as the Occaſion offers; the Servants ſtanding round all the while in a great number, and with the profoundeſt reſpect, ſilence and order imaginable. When you have talked over your Buſineſs, or the Complements, or whatever other Concern brought you thither, he makes a Sign to have things ſerv'd in for the Entertainment; which is generally a little Sweetmeat, a diſh of Sherbet, and another of Coffee: All which are immediately brought in by the Servants, and tender'd to all the Gueſts in order, with the greateſt Care and Awfulneſs imaginable. And they have reaſon to look well to it; for ſhould any Servant make but the leaſt Slip or Miſtake, either in delivering or receiving his Diſh, it might coſt him fifty, perhaps one hundred Drubs on his bare feet, to attone for his Crime. At laſt comes the finiſhing part of your Entertainment, which is perfuming the Beards of the Company; a Ceremony, which is perform'd in this manner. They have for this purpoſe a ſmall Silver Chaffing-diſh, cover'd with a lid full of holes, and fixed upon a handſome Plate. In this they put ſome freſh Coals, and upon them a piece of Lignum Aloes, and then ſhutting it up, the ſmoak immediately aſcends with a grateful Odour thro' the holes of the Cover. This ſmoak is held under every one's Chin, and offer'd as it were a Sacrifice to his Beard. The briſtly Idol ſoon perceives the reverence done to it, and ſo greedily takes in and incorporates the gummy ſteam, that it retains the ſavour of it, and may ſerve for a Noſegay a good while after.

This Ceremony may perhaps ſeem ridiculous at firſt hearing: But it paſſes among the Turks for an high Gratification.

tification. And I will ſay this in its vindication, that its deſign is very wiſe and uſeful. For it is underſtood to give a civil diſmiſſion to the Viſitants; intimating to them, that the Maſter of the Houſe has Buſineſs to do, or ſome other Avocation, that permits them to go away aſſoon as they pleaſe, and the ſooner after this Ceremony the better. By this means you may, at any time, without offence, deliver your ſelf from being detain'd from your Affairs by tedious and unſeaſonable Viſits; and from being conſtrain'd to uſe that piece of Hypocriſy, ſo common in the World, of preſſing thoſe to ſtay longer with you, whom perhaps in your heart you wiſh a great way off for having troubled you ſo long already. But of this enough.

Having diſcharged our viſit to *Oſtan Baſſa* we rid out after Dinner to view the Marine. It is about half an hour diſtant from the City. The Port is an open Sea, rather than an enclos'd Harbour: However it is in part defended from the force of the Waves, by two ſmall Iſlands about two leagues out from the Shore; One of which is call'd the *Bird*, the other the *Coney Iſland*, being ſo named from the Creatures which they ſeverally produce. For its ſecurity from Pyrates, it has ſeveral Caſtles or rather ſquare Towers, built all-along upon the Shore at convenient diſtances. They are (I think) ſix in number, but at preſent void of all manner of force both of Men and Ammunition.

In the Fields near the Shore appear'd many heaps of Ruins and Pillars of Granite, and ſeveral other Indications that here muſt have been anciently ſome conſiderable Buildings this way. Which agrees very well with what *Caſaubon* in his Notes upon *Strabo* (p. 213.) quotes out of *Diodorus*, *viz.* that the place call'd *Tripoli*, was anciently a Cluſter of three Cities ſtanding at a furlong's diſtance from each other; of which the firſt was a Seat of the *Aradii*, the ſecond of the *Sidonians*, the third of the *Tyrians*. And from hence it is probable, that *Tripoli* was a Name given at firſt to three diſtinct, but adjacent places, and not to one City; built (as is uſually ſaid) by the mingled

mingled intereſt of *Tyre*, *Sidon*, and *Aradus*: It being hard to conceive, how three ſuch independent Commonwealths ſhould thus concur in the Founding of one City between them; and harder, how they ſhould agree in governing it afterward.

Sunday, *Mar*. 14.

We continued ſtill in *Tripoli*.

Monday Mar. 15.

Reſolving to proſecute our Journey this day, we had given orders to our Muletiers ſome time before, to be ready to attend us. But they had been ſo frighted by the *Baſſa* of *Sidon*'s Servants, who were abroad in queſt of Mules, for the ſervice of their Maſter, that they were run away, and could not be heard of. A Diſappointment which gave us much Vexation, and left us no other remedy, but only to ſupply our ſelves with freſh Beaſts, where we could find them.

Having after much trouble, put our ſelves in a new poſture of Travelling, we parted from *Tripoli* at three of the Clock in the Afternoon; proceeding cloſe by the Sea, we came in one hour and a half to *Callemone*, a ſmall Village juſt under *Bell-Mount*. From hence putting forward till near eight of the Clock, we came to an high Promontory, which lay directly croſs our way, and broke off abruptly at the Sea ſide, with a Cape very high, and almoſt perpendicular. In order to paſs this Barrier, we turn'd up on the left hand, into a narrow Valley thro' which our Road lay; and it being now late, we took up our Quarters there under ſome Olive Trees, having come in all about five hours.

The Promontory which terminated our Journey, ſeems to be that called by * *Strabo* τὸ τῦ Θεῦ πρόσωπον, or *the face of God*, aſſign'd by that Author for the end of Mount *Libanus*. Between this place and *Tripoli* he mentions likewiſe a City called *Trieris*: But of this we ſaw no Footſteps,

* *Strab.* lib. 16. *Pomp. Mela,* lib. 1. cap. 12.

steps, unless you will allow for such, some Sepulchers which we saw cut in the Rocks, about one hour and a half before we arrived at the Promontory.

Tuesday, *Mar.* 16.

We were no sooner in motion this Morning, but we were engaged in the difficult work of crossing over the forementioned Cape. The Pass over it lies about a mile up from the Sea. We found it very steep and rugged; but in an hour or thereabout master'd it, and arrived in a narrow Valley on the other side, which brought the Sea open to us again. Near the entrance of this Valley stands a small Fort, erected upon a Rock perpendicular on all sides, the Walls of the Buildings being just adequate to the sides of the Rock, and seeming almost of one continued piece with them. This Castle is called *Temseida*, and commands the passage into the Valley.

In about half an hour from this place, we came even with *Patrone*; a place esteem'd to be the antient *Botrus*. It is situate close by the Sea, and our Road lying somewhat higher up in the Land, we diverted a little out of the way to see it. We found in it some remains of an old Church and a Monastery: But these are now perfectly ruin'd and desolate; as is likewise the whole City. Nor is there any thing left in it, to testify it has been a place of any great consideration.

In three hours more we came to *Gibyle*, call'd by the Greeks *Byblus*, a place once famous for the Birth and Temple of *Adonis*. It is pleasantly situated by the Sea side. At present it contains but a little extent of Ground, but yet more than enough for the small number of its Inhabitants. It is compassed with a dry Ditch, and a Wall, with square Towers in it at about every forty yards distance. On its South side it has an old Castle; within it, is a Church, exactly of the same figure with that at *Tortosa*, only not so entire as that. Besides this it has nothing remarkable, tho' anciently it was a place of no mean ex-

 tent,

tent, as well as beauty; as may appear from the many heaps of Ruins, and the fine Pillars that are ſcatter'd up and down in the Gardens near the Town.

Gibyle is probably the Country of the *Giblites*, mention'd *Joſh.* 13.5. King *Hiram* made uſe of the People of this place in preparing Materials for *Solomon*'s Temple; as may be collected from the firſt of *Kings*, 5. 18. where the word which our Tranſlator hath render'd *ſtone-ſquarers* in the Hebrew is גבלים *Giblim*, or *Giblites*, and in the LXXII Interpreters Βύβλιοι, that is the Men of *Byblus*: the former uſing the Hebrew, the latter the Greek Name of this place. The ſame difference may be obſerved likewiſe *Ezek.* 27.9. where this place is again mention'd. The *Ancients of Gebal*, ſays our Tranſlation, following the Hebrew; inſtead of which you read in the LXXII again οἱ πρεσβύτεροι Βυβλίων the Elders of *Bybli* or *Byblus*.

Leaving *Gibyle* we came in one hour to a fair large River, with a Stone Bridge over it, of only one Arch, but that exceeding wide and lofty. To this River the Turks give the Name of *Ibrahim Baſſa*; but it is doubtleſs the ancient River *Adonis*, ſo famous for the Idolatrous Rites perform'd here in lamentation of *Adonis*. Upon the bank of this Stream we took up our Quarters for the following Night, having come this day about ſix hours. We had a very tempeſtuous night both of Wind and Rain, almoſt without ceſſation, and with ſo great violence, that our Servants were hardly able to keep up our Tents over us. But however, this Accident which gave us ſo much trouble in the night, made us amends with a curioſity, which it yielded us an opportunity of beholding the next Morning.

Wedneſday, Mar. 17.

For by this means we had the fortune to ſee what may be ſuppoſed to be the occaſion of that Opinion which *Lucian* relates, concerning this River, *viz.* That this Stream, at certain ſeaſons of the Year, eſpecially about the Feaſt of *Adonis*, is of a bloody colour; which the Heathens

Heathens looked upon as proceeding from a kind of Sympathy in the River, for the Death of *Adonis*, who was killed by a wild Boar in the Mountains, out of which this Stream rises. Something like this we saw actually come to pass; for the Water was stain'd to a surprising redness; and, as we observ'd in Travelling, had discolour'd the Sea a great way into a reddish hue, occasion'd doubtless by a sort of Minium, or red Earth, washed into the River by the violence of the Rain, and not by any stain from *Adonis*'s Blood.

In an hour and a quarter from this River we passed over the foot of the Mountain *Climax*, where, having gone thro' a very rugged and uneven Pass, we came into a large Bay called *Junia*. At the first entrance into the Bay, is an old Stone Bridge, which appoints the limits between the two Bassalicks of *Tripoli* and *Sidon*. At the bottom of the Bay are exceeding high and steep Mountains, between which and the Sea, the Road lies. These are the Mountains of *Castravan*, chiefly inhabited by Maronites, famous for a growth of excellent Wine. The Maronite Bishop of *Aleppo* has here his residence in a Convent, of which he is the Guardian. We saw many other small Convents on the top of these Mountains. One of which call'd *Oozier* was, as we were here told, in the hands of ten or twelve Latin Fryars. Towards the further side of the Bay, we came to a square Tower or Castle, of which kind there are many all along upon the Coast for several days Journey from this place: They are said to have been built by the Empress *Helena*, for the protection of the Country from *Pirates*. At this Tower is to be paid a fourth * Caphar. It is receiv'd by Maronites, a pack of Rogues more exacting and insolent in their office, than the very Turks themselves. A little beyond this place, we came to a Road cut thro' the Rocks, which brought us out of the Bay, having been one hour and a quarter in compassing it. In an hour more spent upon a very rugged way, close by the Sea, we came to the River *Lycus*, call'd also some-

* Half *per* Franck, quarter *per* Servant.

time *Canis*, and by the Turks at this day *Nahor Kelp*. It derives its Name from an Idol in the form of a Dog or Wolf, which was worſhiped, and is ſaid to have pronounc'd Oracles at this place. The Image is pretended to be ſhewn to Strangers at this day, lying in the Sea with its heels upward: I mean the Body of it; for its Oracular head is reported to have been broken off, and carry'd to *Venice*, where (if fame be true) it may be ſeen at this day.

I know not by what miſtake ſeveral modern Geographers confound this River with *Adonis*, making them to be one and the ſame; whereas the contrary is apparent, both from experimental obſervation, and from the Authority of Ancient Geographers.

This River iſſues into the Sea from between two Mountains exceſſive ſteep and high; and ſo rocky that they ſeem to conſiſt each of one entire Stone. For croſſing the River, you go up between theſe Mountains about a Bow ſhot from the Sea, where you have a good Bridge of four Arches; near the foot of which, is a piece of white Marble inlaid in the ſide of a Rock, with an Arab Inſcription on it, intimating its Founder to have been the *Emir Faccardine* (of whom I ſhall have occaſion to ſpeak more when I come to *Beroot*.) Being paſſed the River you immediately begin to aſcend the Mountain, (or rather great Rock) hanging over it on that ſide. To accommodate the paſſage you have a path of above two yards breadth cut along its ſide, at a great height above the Water; being the work of the Emperour *Antoninus*. For the Promontory allowing no Paſſage between it and the Sea, at bottom, that Emperour undertook with incredible labour, to open this way above. The memory of which good work is perpetuated by an Inſcription engraven on a Table plain'd in the ſide of the natural Rock, not far from the entrance into the way. As follows,

IMP:

IMP: CAES: M: AURELIUS
ANTONINUS, PIUS, FELIX, AUGUSTUS
PARTH: MAX: BRIT: GERM: MAXIMUS
PONTIFEX MAXIMUS
MONTIBUS IMMINENTIBUS
LYCO FLUMINI CAESIS VIAM DILATAVIT
PER---- (*purposely erased*) ----
ANTONINIANAM SUAM

A little higher up in the way are inſcrib'd theſe words

INVICTE IMP: ANTONINE P: FELIX AUG:
MULTIS ANNIS IMPERA!

In paſſing this way, we obſerv'd, in the ſides of the Rock above us, ſeveral Tables of figures carv'd; which ſeem'd to promiſe ſomething of Antiquity. To be ſatisfied of which, ſome of us clamber'd up to the place, and found there ſome ſigns as if the old way had gone in that Region, before *Antoninus* cut the other more convenient paſſage a little lower. In ſeveral places hereabouts, we ſaw ſtrange antique figures of Men, carv'd in the natural Rock, in Mezzo Relievo, and in bigneſs equal to the life. Cloſe by each figure was a large Table plain'd in the ſide of the Rock, and border'd round with Mouldings. Both the Effigies and the Tables appear'd to have been anciently inſcrib'd all over: But the characters are now ſo defac'd, that nothing but the footſteps of them were viſible. Only there was one of the figures that had both its lineaments and its Inſcriptions entire.

It was our unhappineſs to have at this place a very violent ſtorm of Thunder and Rain, which made our Company too much in haſte to make any long ſtay here. By which misfortune I was prevented to my great Regret, from copying the Inſcription, and making ſuch an exact ſcrutiny

ſcrutiny into this Antiquity as it ſeem'd very well to deſerve. I hope ſome curious Traveller or other will have better ſucceſs in paſſing this way hereafter. The Figures ſeem'd to reſemble Mummys, and were perhaps the repreſentation of ſome perſons buried hereabout; whoſe Sepulchers might probably alſo be diſcover'd by the diligent Obſerver.

The *Antonine* way extends about a quarter of an hours Travel. It is at preſent ſo broken and uneven, that, to repair it, would require no leſs labour, than that, wherewith it was at firſt made. After this Paſs you come upon a ſmooth ſandy Shore, which brings you in about one hour and a half to the River *Beroot*, (for I could learn no other Name it had:) It is a large River, and has over it a Stone Bridge of ſix Arches. On its other ſide is a plain Field near the Sea, which is ſaid to be the Stage on which St *George* duell'd and kill'd the Dragon. In memory of this Atchievement, there is a ſmall Chappel built upon the place, dedicated at firſt to that Chriſtian Hero; but now perverted to a Moſque. From hence in an hour we arrived at *Beroot*, very wet by reaſon of the long and ſevere Rain. However we found here the ſhelter of a good *Kane* by the Sea ſide, and there we took up our Quarters. Our whole Stage this day was about ſix hours and a half.

Thurſday, March 18.

The day following we ſpent at *Beroot*; being credibly inform'd that the River *Damer*, which lay in our next Stage, was ſo ſwoln by the late Rains that it would be impaſſable. This place was call'd anciently *Berytus*; from which the Idol *Baal Berith* is ſuppoſed to have had its Name. And afterwards being greatly eſteem'd by *Auguſtus*, had many Privileges confer'd upon it; and together with them a new Name, *viz. Julia Felix.* But at preſent, it retains nothing of its ancient felicity, except the ſituation; and in that particular it is indeed very happy. It is ſeated on the Sea-ſide, in a ſoil fertile and delightful, rais'd only ſo high above the ſalt Water, as to be ſecure from

EMIR FECHRREDDIN, Prince der Drusen. *Pag.* 293.

[illegible] mountains. But besides these advantages of its situation, it has at present nothing else to boast of.

from its overflowings, and all other noxious and unwholsome effects of that Element. It has the benefit of good fresh Springs flowing down to it from the adjacent Hills, and dispensed all over the City, in convenient, and not unhandsome Fountains. But besides these advantages of its situation, it has at present nothing else to boast of.

The *Emir Faccardine* had his chief residence in this place. He was in the Reign of *Sultan Morat*, the fourth *Emir*, or Prince of the *Druses*; a people suppos'd to have descended from some dispers'd remainders of those Christian Armies, that engaged in the Crusades, for the recovery of the *Holy-Land*: Who afterwards, being totally routed, and despairing of a return to their native Country again, betook themselves to the Mountains hereabout; in which their descendants have continued ever since. *Faccardine* being (as I said) Prince of these People, was not contented to be penn'd up in the Mountains; but by his power and artifice, enlarged his Dominions down into the plain all along the Sea Coast as far as from this place to *Acra*. At last the Grand Seignior grown jealous of such a growing power, drove the wild Beast back again to the Mountains, from whence he had broke loose; and there his posterity retain their Principality to this day.

We went to view the Palace of this Prince, which stands on the North East part of the City. At the entrance of it is a Marble Fountain, of greater beauty than is usually seen in *Turkey*. The Palace within consists of several Courts, all now run much to ruin; or rather perhaps never finish'd. The Stables, Yards for Horses, Dens for Lyons and other Salvage Creatures, Gardens, *&c.* are such as would not be unworthy of the Quality of a Prince in Christendom, were they wrought up to that perfection of which they are capable, and to which they seem to have been design'd by their first Contriver.

But the best sight that this palace affords, and the worthiest to be remember'd, is the Orange Garden. It contains a large Quadrangular plat of ground, divided into sixteen lesser squares, four in a row, with walks between them.

The

The walks are ſhaded with Orange Trees, of a large ſpreading ſize, and all of ſo fine a growth both for ſtem and head, that one cannot imagine any thing more perfect in this kind. They were, at the time when we were there, as it were, guilded with Fruit, hanging thicker upon them than ever I ſaw Apples in *England*. Every one of theſe ſixteen leſſer ſquares in the Garden was border'd with ſtone; and in the ſtone-work were Troughs very Artificially contriv'd, for conveying the Water all over the Garden: There being little Outlets cut at every Tree, for the Stream, as it paſs'd by, to flow out, and water it. Were this place under the Cultivation of an Engliſh Gardner, it is impoſſible any thing could be made more delightful. But theſe *Heſperides* were put to no better uſe, when we ſaw them, than to ſerve as a fold for Sheep and Goats; inſomuch that in many places they were up to the knees in dirt: So little ſenſe have the Turks of ſuch refin'd delights as theſe; being a people generally of the groſſeſt apprehenſion, and knowing few other pleaſures, but ſuch ſenſualities, as are equally common both to Men and Beaſts. On the Eaſt ſide of this Garden were two Terrace walks riſing one above the other, each of them having an aſcent to it of twelve ſteps. They had both ſeveral fine ſpreading Orange Trees upon them, to make ſhades in proper places. And at the North end they led into Booths, and Summer-houſes, and other Apartments very delightful: this place being deſign'd by *Faccardine* for the chief ſeat of his pleaſure.

In may perhaps be wonder'd, how this *Emir* ſhould be able to contrive any thing ſo elegant and regular as this Garden; ſeeing the Turkiſh Gardens are uſually nothing elſe but a confus'd miſcellany of Trees, jumbled together without either Knots, Walks, Arbours, or any thing of art or deſign, ſo that they ſeem like Thickets rather than Gardens. But *Faccardine* had been in *Italy*, where he had ſeen things of another nature, and knew well how to copy them in his own Country. For indeed it appears by theſe remains of him, that he muſt needs have been a Man much above the ordinary level of a Turkiſh Genius.

In

In another Garden we ſaw ſeveral Pedeſtals for Statues; from whence it may be inferr'd, that this *Emir* was no very zealous *Mahometan*. At one Corner of the ſame Garden ſtood a Tower of about ſixty foot high; deſign'd to have been carried to a much greater elevation for a Watch-Tower, and for that end built with an extraordinary ſtrength, its walls being twelve foot thick. From this Tower we had a view of the whole City: Amongſt other Proſpects it yielded us the ſight of a large Chriſtian Church, ſaid to have been at firſt conſecrated to St *John* the *Evangeliſt*. But, it being now uſurp'd by the Turks for their chief Moſque, we could not be permitted to ſee it, otherwiſe than at this diſtance. Another Church there is in the Town, which ſeems to be ancient; but being a very mean Fabrick is ſuffer'd to remain ſtill in the hands of the *Greeks*. We found it adorn'd with abundance of old Pictures; Amongſt the reſt I ſaw one with this little Inſcription, Κούαρτος πρεσῶτος Αρχιεπίσκοπος Βηρύτου: And juſt by it was the figure of *Neſtorius*, who commonly makes one amongſt the Saints painted in the Greek Churches; tho' they do not now profeſs, nor, I believe, ſo much as know his Hereſy. But that which appear'd moſt obſervable was a very odd figure of a Saint, drawn at full length, with a large Beard reaching down to his feet. The Curate gave us to underſtand that this was St *Nicephorus*; and perceiving that his Beard was the chief object of our admiration, he gratified us with the following relation concerning him, *viz*. That he was a Perſon of the moſt Eminent Virtues in his time. But his great Miſfortune was, that the Endowments of his Mind were not ſet off with the outward Ornament of a Beard. Upon occaſion of which defect, he fell into a deep Melancholy. The Devil taking the advantage of this Prieſt, promiſed to give him that Boon which Nature had deny'd, in caſe he would comply with his ſuggeſtions. The Beardleſs Saint, tho' he was very deſirous of the reward propos'd, yet he would not purchaſe it at that rate neither: But rejected the previous Bribe with indignation, declaring

F reſo-

resolutely, that he had rather for ever despair of his wish than obtain it upon such terms. And at the same time, taking in his hand the downy tuft upon his Chin, to witness the stability of his resolution (for he had it seems Beard enough to swear by) Behold! as a reward for his constancy, he found the hair immediately stretch, with the pluck that he gave it. Whereupon finding it in so good a humour, he follow'd the happy Omen: And as young Heirs that have been niggardly bred, generally turn Prodigals when they come to their Estates; so he never desisted from pulling his Beard, till he had wiredrawn it down to his Feet. But enough both of the beard and the story. At the East end of *Beroot* are to be seen seven or eight beautiful Pillars of Granite, each —— foot long, and three in diameter. And over another Gate, not far distant, we found in a piece of Marble, this following Inscription; Τῆς τοῦ προσιόντος ἀνδρὸς ἐννοίας αἰεὶ σαφὴς ἔλεγχος, ἡ πρόσοψις γείνεται δίδου προθυμῶς ὃ παρέχεις ἢ μὴ δίδου παρὰ γὰρ τὸ μειζὸν γείνεται πλήρης χάρις. ΤΗΣ ΤΟΥ ΠΡΟΣΙΟΝΤΟΣ ΑΝΔΡΟΣ ΕΝΝΟΙΑΣ. Such as these were the Capitals. It was probably at first an Altar-Inscription, relating to the Offertory in the Holy Communion: For its sense seems to look that way; and 'tis well known that the Comers to the Blessed Sacrament, were call'd by the Ancients, by the peculiar Name of οἱ προσιόντες, as *Valesius* proves out of St *Chrysostom. Vales. Not.* in *Euseb. Eccl. Hist. Lib. 7. Cap. 9.*

On the South side, the Town-wall is still entire, but built out of the ruins of the old City, as appears by pieces of Pillars and Marble, which help to build it. In one piece of Marble Table we saw these remaining Letters of a Latin Inscription;

---- VG. ETIA ----
---- XI CUM ----
---- VS PHOBBUS ----

All the rest being purposely erased.

A little

A little without this Wall, we saw many Granite Pillars and remnants of Mosaick Floors; and in an heap of rubbish, several pieces of polish'd Marble, fragments of Statues, and other poor Relicks of this City's ancient Magnificence. On the Sea side is an old ruin'd Castle, and some remains of a small Mole.

Friday, Mar. 19.

Leaving *Beroot*, we came in one third of an hour to a large Plain extending from the Sea to the Mountains. At the beginning of the Plain is a Grove of Pine Trees of *Faccardine*'s Plantation. We guess'd it to be more than half a Mile cross; and so pleasant, and inviting was its shade, that it was not without some regret that we pass'd it by. Continuing in this Plain, we saw at a distance, on our left hand, a small Village called *Suckfoat*. It belongs to the *Druses*, who possess at this day a long tract of Mountains, as far as from *Castravan* to *Carmel*. Their present Prince is *Achmet*, Grandson to *Faccardine*; an old Man, and one who keeps up the Custom of his Ancestors, of turning day into night: An hereditary practice in his Family, proceeding from a traditional perswasion amongst them, that Princes can never sleep securely but by day, when Mens actions and designs are best observ'd by their Guards, and if need be, most easily prevented; but that in the night it concerns them to be always vigilant, lest the darkness, aided by their sleeping, should give Traitors both opportunity and encouragement to assault their Persons, and by a Dagger or a Pistol, to make them continue their sleep longer than they intended when they lay down.

Two hours from *Faccardine*'s Grove brought us to the fifth Caphar, and another little hour to the River *Damer* or *Tamyras*; the former being its Modern, the latter its Ancient Name. It is a River apt to swell much upon sudden Rains, in which case, precipitating its self from the Mountains with great rapidity, it has been fatal to many a Passenger; amongst the rest, one Monsieur *Spon*, Nephew to Dr *Spon*, coming from *Jerusalem*, about four years ago, in company with ſome Engliſh Gentlemen, was, in paſſing this Stream, hurry'd down by it, and periſhed in the Sea, which lies about a furlong lower than the Paſſage.

We had the good fortune to find the River in a better temper; its waters being now aſſwaged ſince the late Rains. However the Country Fellows were ready here, according to their Trade, to have aſſiſted us in our paſſing over. In order to which, they had very officiouſly ſtripp'd themſelves naked againſt our coming: And to the end that they might oblige us to make uſe of their help, for which they will be well paid, they brought us to a place where the Water was deepeſt, pretending there was no other Paſſage beſides that; which Cheat we ſaw them actually impoſe upon ſome other Travellers, who came not long after us. But we had been advis'd of a place a little higher in the River, where the Stream was broader and ſhallower, and there we eaſily paſs'd without their aſſiſtance. Juſt by this place are the ruins of a Stone-bridge; of which one might gueſs by the firmneſs of its remains, that it might have been ſtill entire, had not theſe Villains broke it down in order to their making their advantages of Paſſengers; either conducting them over for good pay, or elſe, if they have opportunity, drowning them for their ſpoils.

On the other ſide of the River, the Mountains approach cloſer to the Sea, leaving only a narrow rocky way between. From *Damer*, in two hours we came to another River, of no inconſiderable figure, but not once mention'd by any Geographer that I know of. It is within one hour of *Sidon*. Its Channel is deep, contains a good Stream, and has a large Stone-bridge over it. Speaking of this River to the Reverend Father *Stephano*, Maronite Patriarch at *Canobine*, he told me it was call'd *Awle*, and had its Fountain near *Berook*, a Village in Mount *Libanus*.

At this River we were met by ſeveral of the French Merchants from *Sidon*; they having a Factory there the moſt conſiderable of all theirs in the *Levant*. Being arriv'd at *Sidon*, we pitch'd our Tents by a Ciſtern without the

the City; but were our selves conducted by the French Gentlemen to the place of their habitation, which is a large *Kane* close by the Sea, where the Consul and all the Nation are quarter'd together. Before the front of this *Kane* is an old Mole running into the Sea with a right Angle; it was of no great capacity at best, but now is render'd perfectly useless, having been purposely fill'd up with rubbish and earth, by *Faccardine*, to prevent the Turkish Gallies from making their unwelcome visits to this place. The Mole being thus destroy'd, all Ships, that take in their Burthen here, are forced to ride at Anchor under the shelter of a small ridge of Rocks, about a Mile distant from the shore on the North side of the City. *Sidon* is stockt well enough with Inhabitants, but is very much shrunk from its ancient extent, and more from its splendour; As appears from a great many beautiful Pillars, that lie scatter'd up and down the Gardens without the present Walls. Whatever Antiquities may at any time have been hereabout, they are now all perfectly obscur'd and buried by the Turkish Buildings. Upon the South side of the City, on a Hill stands an old Castle, said to have been the work of *Lewis* the ninth of *France*, surnamed the *Saint*; and not far from the Castle is an old unfinish'd Palace of *Faccardine*'s, serving however the *Bassa* for his Seraglio: Neither of them worth mentioning, had the City afforded us any thing else more remarkable. Near about *Sidon* begin the precincts of the *Holy Land*, and of that part of it in particular which was allotted to *Asher*. The borders of which Tribe extended from *Carmel* as far as great *Zidon*, as appears from *Josh*. 19. 26, 28. But the People upon the Sea Coasts were never actually master'd by the *Israelites*; being left by the just Judgment of God to be thorns in their sides, for a reason that may be seen *Jud*. 2. 1, 2, 3, &c.

The Person, who is the French Consul at *Sidon*, has also the Title of Consul of *Jerusalem*; and is obliged by his Master, the French King, to make a visit to the Holy City every Easter, under pretence of preserving the Sanctuary

ctuary there from the violations, and the Fryars who have the custody of it, from the exactions of the Turks. But the Friars think themselves much safer without this protection. We were desirous to joyn with Monsieur *l'Empereur*, the present Consul, in his this years Pilgrimage; and accordingly had sent him a Letter from *Aleppo* on purpose to bespeak that favour; hoping by his protection to pass more securely from the abuses of the Arabs and Turks, who are no where so insolent, as in *Palestine*, and about *Jerusalem*. We had his promise to stay for us; but the remoras and disappointments we met with in the Road, had put us so backward in our Journey, that fearing to be too late at *Jerusalem*, he set out from *Sidon* the day before our arrival there: Leaving us however some hopes, that if we made the best of our way, we might come up with him at *Acra*, where he promis'd to expect our coming to the utmost moment.

Saturday, *Mar*. 20.

Being desirous therefore not to lose the convenience of his company, we set out early the next morning from *Sidon*; and travelling in a very fruitful Plain, came in half an hour to a place where we found a large Pillar of Granite, lying cross the high way, and sunk a good part under ground. Observing some letters upon it, we took the pains to dig away the Earth, by which means we recover'd this fragment of an Inscription.

IMPE-

IMPERATORES,
CAESARES,
L SEPTIMUS SE-
VERUS, PIUS PER-
TINAX, AUG: ARA-
BICUS ADIABENICUS,
PARTHICUS, MAXI-
MUS, TRIBUNICIA
POTES: VI. IMP: XI. COS []
PRO ❧ COS ❧ P ❧ P
ET M ❧ AUREL: ANTONI-
NUS AUG: FILIUS ❧ EJUS
-------------ET-----ARIA
--------EN----ƆIUM ❧ RV
FVM---------------------
-------IC PR: PRAET
----PROVINC ❧ SYRIAE
[ET PHAE] NIC ❧ RENOVAVERUNT
❧ [] ❧

Some Gentlemen of our Nation, in their Journey to *Jeruſalem*, this laſt Eaſter, *An.* 1699. found another Pillar, at about midway, between that we ſaw, and *Sidon*, of the ſame make and uſe; from which they took the foreſaid Inſcription more perfectly. As far as *filius ejus* there is no variation, and after that it goes on thus,

VIAS ET MILLIARIA
FR---O ❧ VENIDIVM RV
FVM ❧ LEG ❧ AUGG ❧
L----PR ❧ PRAESIDEM
PROVINC ❧ SYRIAEPHOE
NIC ❧ RENOVAVERUNT
❧ I ❧

By which we may obſerve the exactneſs of the Romans in meaſuring out their Roads, and marking down upon every Pillar the number of Miles as I. II. III. *&c.*

A little

A little beyond this Pillar, we paſſed in ſight of *Ko-ri-e*, a large Village on the ſide of the Mountains; and in two hours and a half more, came to *Sarphan*, ſuppos'd to be the Ancient *Serephath*, or *Sarepta*, ſo famous for the reſidence and Miracles of the Prophet *Elijah*. The place ſhewn us for this City, conſiſted of only a few Houſes, on the tops of the Mountains, within about half a Mile of the Sea. But it is more probable, the principal part of the City ſtood below, in the ſpace between the Hills and the Sea; there being ruins ſtill to be ſeen in that place of a conſiderable extent. From hence in three hours we arrived at *Caſimeer*, a River large and deep, running down to the Sea thro' a Plain, in which it creeps along with various mæanders and turnings. It had once a good Stone-bridge laid over it of four Arches: But of that nothing remains at preſent, except the ſupporters; between which there are laid beams and boards to ſupply the room of the Arches, and to make a Paſſage over. But ſo careleſs and looſe is the Fabrick, that it looks like a trap rather than a Bridge. We had one Horſe dropt thro', notwithſtanding our utmoſt care to prevent ſuch misfortunes. But 'twas our good luck to recover him again ſafe a-ſhore.

This River is aſſign'd by our Modern Geographers for the old *Eleutherus*; but how erroneouſly, has been aforemention'd. *Strabo* mentions a certain River falling into the Sea near *Tyre*, on this ſide (πρὸς Τύρῳ Ποταμὸς ἐξίησι. p. 521.) which can be no other than this; but he omits to acquaint us with its Name. Within a Bow ſhot of the River *Caſimeer* is a *Kane* of the ſame Name, from which, keeping near the Sea ſide, you arrive in an hour at *Tyre*.

This City, ſtanding in the Sea upon a Peninſula, promiſes at a diſtance ſomething very magnificent. But when you come to it, you find no ſimilitude of that Glory, for which it was ſo renown'd in ancient times, and which the Prophet *Ezekiel* deſcribes, *Chap.* 26, 27, 28. On the North ſide it has an old Turkiſh ungarriſon'd Caſtle; beſides which, you ſee nothing here, but a mere *Babel* of broken Walls, Pillars, Vaults, *&c.* there being not ſo much

as

as one entire House left. Its present Inhabitants are only a few poor wretches, harbouring themselves in the Vaults, and subsisting chiefly upon fishing; who seem to be preserv'd in this place by Divine Providence, as a visible argument, how God has fulfill'd his Word concerning *Tyre*, *viz*. *That it should be as the top of a rock, a place for fishers to dry their nets on*, *Ezek*. 26. 14.

In the midst of the Ruins, there stands up, one pile, higher than the rest, which is the East end of a great Church, probably of the Cathedral of *Tyre*: And why not the very same that was erected by its Bishop *Paulinus*, and honour'd with that famous Consecration-Sermon of *Eusebius*, recorded by himself in his *Eccl. Hist. Lib.* 10. *Cap.* 4. this having been an Archiepiscopal See in the Christian times?

I cannot, in this place, omit an observation made by most of our Company in this Journey, *viz*. That in all the ruins of Churches which we saw, tho' their other parts were totally demolish'd, yet the East end we always found standing, and tolerably entire. Whether the Christians, when over-run by Infidels, redeem'd their Altars from ruin with Money; or whether, even the Barbarians, when they demolished the other parts of the Churches, might voluntarily spare these, out of an Awe and Veneration; or whether they have stood thus long, by virtue of some peculiar firmness in the nature of their Fabrick; or whether some occult Providence has preserv'd them, as so many standing Monuments of Christianity in these unbelieving Regions, and presages of its future Restauration, I will not determine. This only I will say, that we found it in fact, so as I describ'd, in all the ruin'd Churches that came in our way; being perhaps not fewer than one hundred: nor do I remember ever to have seen one instance of the contrary. This might justly seem a trifling observation, were it founded upon a few examples only. But it being a thing so often, and indeed universally observ'd by us, throughout our whole Journey, I thought it must needs proceed from something more than blind chance, and might very well deserve this Animadversion.

But to return from this digreſſion; There being an old Stair-caſe in this ruin laſt mention'd, I got up to the top of it: From whence I had an entire Proſpect of the Iſland, part of *Tyre*, of the Iſthmus, and of the adjacent ſhore. I thought I could from this Elevation diſcern the Iſthmus to be a Soil of a different Nature from the other two; it lying lower than either, and being cover'd all over with ſand which the Sea caſts upon it, as the tokens of its natural right to a Paſſage there, from which it was by *Alexander* the Great injuriouſly excluded. The Iſland of *Tyre* in its natural ſtate, ſeems to have been of a circular figure, containing not more than forty Acres of Ground. It diſcovers ſtill the foundations of a Wall, which anciently encompaſs'd it round, at the outmoſt margin of the Land. It makes, with the Iſthmus, two large Bays; one on its North ſide, and the other on its South. Theſe Bays are, in part, defended from the Ocean, each by a long Ridge, reſembling a Mole, ſtretching directly out, on both ſides, from the head of the Iſland; but theſe ridges, whether they were Walls or Rocks, whether the work of Art or Nature, I was too far diſtant to diſcern.

Coming out of theſe ruins, we ſaw the foundation of a very ſtrong Wall, running croſs the Neck of Land, and ſerving as a Barrier, to ſecure the City on this ſide. From this place, we were one third of an hour in paſſing the ſandy Iſthmus, before we came to the ground, which we apprehended to be the natural ſhore. From hence paſſing over part of a very fertile Plain, which extends its ſelf to a vaſt compaſs before *Tyre*, we arrived in three quarters of an hour at *Roſelayn*. Our whole Stage from *Sidon* hither was about eight hours.

Sunday, Mar. 21.

Roſelayn is a place where are the Ciſterns called *Solomon*'s, ſuppoſed, according to the common tradition hereabouts, to have been made by that great King, as part of his recompence to King *Hiram*, for the ſupplies of materials, ſent by him toward the building of the Temple.

They

Solomon'

sterns Pag. 51
MB. f.

They are doubtleſs very ancient, but yet of a much later date, than what this tradition aſcribes to them. That they could not be built till ſince *Alexander*'s time, may be conjectur'd from this, amongſt other arguments; becauſe the Aqueduct, which conveys the Water from hence to *Tyre*, is carried over the Neck of Land, by which *Alexander* in his famous Siege of this place joyn'd the City to the Continent. And as the Ciſterns cannot well be imagin'd to be ancienter than the Aqueduct; ſo one may be ſure the Aqueduct cannot be older than the ground it ſtands upon. Of theſe Ciſterns there are three entire at this day, one about a furlong and a half diſtant from the Sea, the other two a little farther up.

The former is of an Octogonal figure, twenty two yards in diameter. It is elevated above the ground nine yards on the South ſide, and ſix on the North; and within, is ſaid to be of an unfathomable deepneſs, but ten yards of line confuted that opinion. Its Wall is of no better a material than Gravel and ſmall Pebles; but conſolidated with ſo ſtrong and tenacious a cement, that it ſeems to be all one entire veſſel of Rock. Upon the brink of it you have a walk round, eight foot broad. From which, deſcending by one ſtep on the South ſide, and by two on the North, you have another walk twenty one foot broad. All this Structure, tho' ſo broad at top, is yet made hollow, ſo that the Water comes in underneath the walks; inſomuch that I could not with a long rod reach the extremity of the cavity. The whole Veſſel contains a vaſt Body of excellent Water; and is ſo well ſupply'd from its Fountain, that tho' there iſſues from it a ſtream like a Brook, driving four Mills between this place and the Sea, yet it is always brim full. On the Eaſt ſide of this Ciſtern was the ancient outlet of the Water, by an Aqueduct raiſed about ſix yards from the ground, and containing a Channel one yard wide. But this is now ſtopp'd up, and dry; the Turks having broke an outlet on the other ſide, deriving thence a ſtream for grinding their Corn.

The Aqueduct (now dry) is carried Eaſtward about one

hundred and twenty paces, and then approaches the two other Cisterns, of which one is twelve, the other twenty yards square. These have each a little Channel, by which they anciently render'd their Waters into the Aqueduct; and so the united streams of all the three Cisterns were carried together to *Tyre*. You may trace out the Aqueduct all along, by the remaining fragments of it. It goes about one hour Northward, and then turning to the West, at a small Mount where anciently stood a Fort, but now a Mosque, it proceeds over the Isthmus into the City. As we pass'd by the Aqueduct, we observ'd in several places on its sides, and under its Arches, rugged heaps of matter resembling Rocks. These were produced by the leakage of the Water, which petrify'd as it distill'd from above; and by the continual adherence of new matter, were grown to a large bulk. That which was most remarkable in them, was the frame and configuration of their parts. They were compos'd of innumerable tubes of Stone, of different sizes, cleaving to one another like Icicles. Each tube had a small cavity in its Center, from which its parts were projected in form of rays, to the circumference, after the manner of the Stones vulgarly call'd Thunder-stones.

The Fountain of these Waters is as unknown as the Contriver of them. It is certain from their rising so high, they must be brought from some part of the Mountains, which are about a league distant; and 'tis as certain that the work was well done at first, seeing it performs its office so well, at so great a distance of time.

Leaving this pleasant Quarter, we came in an hour and half to the white Promontory; so call'd from the aspect it yields towards the Sea. Over this you pass by a way of about two yards broad, cut along its side; from which the prospect down is very dreadful, by reason of the extream depth and steepness of the Mountain, and the raging of the waves at bottom. This way is about one third of an hour over, and is said to have been the work of *Alexander* the Great. About one third of an hour farther, you pass by an heap of rubbish close by the Sea side, being

being the ruins of the Castle *Scandalium*; taking its Name from its Founder, the same *Alexander*, whom the Turks call *Scander*. The ruin is one hundred and twenty paces square, having a dry ditch encompassing it; and from under it, on the side next the Sea, there issues out a Fountain of very fair Water. In an hour from hence you come to the sixth Caphar, called *Nachera*. And in another hour to the Plain of *Acra*, over a very deep and rugged Mountain, supposed to be part of *Mount-Saron*. All the way from the white Promontory to this Plain is exceeding rocky; but here the pleasantness of the Road makes you amends for the former labour.

The Plain of *Acra* extends its self in length from *Mount-Saron* as far as *Carmel*, which is at least six good hours; and in breadth, between the Sea and the Mountains, it is in most places two hours over. It enjoys good streams of Water at convenient distances, and every thing else, that might render it both pleasant and fruitful. But this delicious Plain is now almost desolate; being suffer'd, for want of culture, to run up to rank weeds, which were, at the time when we pass'd it, as high as our Horses backs.

Having Travelled about one hour in the Plain of *Acra*, we passed by an old Town call'd *Zib*, situate on an ascent close by the Sea side. This may probably be the old *Achzib*. mention'd *Josh*. 19. 29. and *Jud*. 1. 31. called afterwards *Ecdippa*: For St *Jerome* places *Achzib* nine Miles distant from *Ptolemais* toward *Tyre*, to which account we found the situation of *Zib* exactly agreeing. This is one of the places, out of which the *Ashurites* could not expel the *Canaanitish* Natives. Two hours farther we came to a Fountain of very good Water, call'd by the French Merchants at *Acra*, *the Fountain of the Blessed Virgin*. In one hour more, we arriv'd at *Acra*. Our whole Stage from *Roselayn* hither was about eight hours and a half.

Acra had anciently the Name of *Accho*, and is another of the places, out of which the Children of Israel could not drive the primitive Inhabitants, *Judg*. 1. 31. Being in after times enlarged by *Ptolemy* the first, it was call'd by him

him, from his own Name *Ptolemais*. But now ſince it hath been in the poſſeſſion of the Turks, it has (according to the example of many other Cities in Turky) caſt of its Greek, and *recover'd ſome ſemblance of its old Hebrew Name again; being called *Acca*, or *Acra*.

This City was for a long time the Theatre of Contention between the Chriſtians and Infidels; till at laſt, after having divers times changed its Maſters, it was by a long Siege finally taken by the Turks, and ruin'd by them in ſuch a manner, as if they had thought, they could never take a full revenge upon it for the blood it had coſt them, or ſufficiently prevent ſuch ſlaughters for the future. As to its ſituation, it enjoys all poſſible advantages both of Sea and Land. On its North and Eaſt ſides it is compaſs'd with a ſpacious and fertile Plain; on the Weſt it is waſhed by the Mediterranean Sea, and on the South by a large Bay, extending from the City as far as *Mount Carmel*.

But notwithſtanding all theſe advantages, it has never been able to recover it ſelf, ſince its laſt fatal overthrow. For beſides a large *Kane* in which the French Factors have taken up their Quarters, and a Moſque, and a few poor Cottages, you ſee nothing here but a vaſt and ſpacious ruin. It is ſuch a ruin however, as ſufficiently demonſtrates the ſtrength of the place in former times. It appears to have been encompaſs'd, on the Land ſide, by a double Wall defended with Towers at ſmall diſtances: And without the Walls are Ditches, Ramparts, and a kind of Baſtions faced with hewn ſtone. In the Fields without theſe works, we ſaw ſcatter'd up and down upon the ground ſeveral large balls of Stone, of at leaſt thirteen or fourteen inches diameter; which were part of the Ammunition uſed in Battering the City, Guns being then unknown. Within the Walls there ſtill appear ſeveral ruins which ſeem to diſtinguiſh themſelves from the general heap, by ſome marks of a greater ſtrength and magnificence. As firſt, thoſe of the

* *Ammian. Marcell.* ſays the Greek and Roman Names of places never took amongſt the Natives of this Country: which is the reaſon that moſt places retain their firſt Oriental Names at this day, *Lib.* 14. *Hiſt. non longe ab initio.*

Cathe-

VVt-legghinge van den H. bergh Carmelus.

1. Den heyligen berg *Carmelus*. 2. Speloncke der oude Vaders. 3. Het out klooster *Seunion* genoemt 4. Fonteyne van *Elias*. 5. Daer het hemels vier op *Elias* brandt-offer viel. 6. Oude ende d'eerste kercke. 7. Kleyne speloncke van *Elias*. 8. Oudt vervallen klooster 9. Klooster van sinte *Theresia*. 10. De groote speloncke van *Elias*. 11. De stadt *Cayphas*. 12. Daer *Elias* dede dooden vier-houdert en vyftigh valsche Propheten. 13. De beke *Cißon*. 14. Daer *Lamech Cain* doodde. Den wegh naer *Israël*.

Mount Carmel *Pag. 54.*

1. The great monastery of the Carmelites. 2. Where Elias sacrific'd 3. The river Kishon. 4 The haven of St. John d'Acre. 5. The town of St. John d'Acra. 6. The river Belus.

Cathedral Church dedicated to St *Andrew*, which ſtands not far from the Sea ſide, more high and conſpicuous than the other ruins. Secondly, the Church of St *John* the tutelar Saint of this City. Thirdly, the Convent of the Knights Hoſpitallers; a place whoſe remaining Walls ſufficiently teſtify its ancient ſtrength. And not far from the Convent, the Palace of the grand Maſter of that Order. The Magnificence of which, may be gueſs'd from a large Stair-caſe, and part of a Church ſtill remaining in it. Fourthly, ſome remains of a large Church formerly belonging to a Nunnery, of which they tell this memorable ſtory. The Turks having preſs'd this City with a long and furious Siege, at laſt enter'd it by Storm, *May* 19. 1291. In which great extremity, the Abbeſs of this Nunnery, fearing leſt ſhe, and thoſe under her care, might be forced to ſubmit to ſuch Beſtialities, as are uſual in caſes of that deplorable Nature, uſed this cruel but generous means for ſecuring both her ſelf and them. She ſummon'd all her flock together, and exhorted them to cut and mangle their faces, as the only way to preſerve their Virgin purity: And to ſhew how much ſhe was in earneſt, ſhe immediately began before them all, to make her ſelf an Example of her own Counſel. The Nuns were ſo animated by this heroical reſolution, and pattern of the Abbeſs, that they began inſtantly to follow her Example, cutting off their Noſes, and disfiguring their faces, with ſuch terrible gaſhes, as might excite horrour rather than luſtful deſires in the Beholders. The conſequence of which was, that the Souldiers breaking into the Nunnery, and ſeeing, inſtead of thoſe beautiful Ladies they expected, ſuch tragical ſpectacles, took a revenge for their diſappointed luſts by putting them all to the Sword. Thus reſtoring them, as in Charity we may ſuppoſe, to a new and inviolable beauty. But to go on; Many other ruins here are of Churches, Palaces, Monaſteries, Forts, *&c.* extending for more than half a Mile in length; in all which you may diſcern marks of ſo much ſtrength, as if every Building in the City had been contriv'd for War and Defence.

But

But that which pleaſed us moſt at *Acra*, was to find the French Conſul Monſieur *l'Empereur* there; who had been ſo generous, as to make a Halt of two days, in expectation of our arrival. But he had ſtaid to the utmoſt extent of his time, and therefore reſolv'd to ſet forward again the next Morning. Our greateſt difficulty was to determine which Road to take, whether that upon the Coaſt by *Cæſarea* and *Joppa*; or that by *Nazareth*, or a middle way between both the other, over the Plain of *Eſdraelon*.

The cauſe of this uncertainty was, the Embroylments and Factions that were then amongſt the Arabs; which made us deſirous to keep as far as poſſible out of their way. 'Tis the policy of the Turks, always to ſow diviſions amongſt theſe wild people, by ſetting up ſeveral heads over their Tribes, often depoſing the old, and placing new ones in their ſtead: By which Art they create contrary Intereſts and Parties amongſt them, preventing them from ever uniting under any one Prince; which if they ſhould have the ſence to do, (being ſo numerous and almoſt the ſole Inhabitants thereabouts) they might ſhake off the Turkiſh yoak, and make themſelves ſupream Lords of the Country.

But however uſeful theſe diſcords may be to the Turks in this reſpect, yet a ſtranger is ſure to ſuffer by them; being made a prey to each Party, according as he happens to come in their way: Avoiding which abuſes, we reſolv'd to take the middle way, as the moſt ſecure at this time.

Monday, Mar. 22.

According to which purpoſe, we ſet out early the next Morning from *Acra*, having with us a band of Turkiſh Souldiers for our ſecurer Convoy. Our Road lay, for about half an hour, along by the ſide of the Bay of *Acra*; and then, arriving at the bottom of the Bay, we turn'd Southward. Here we paſs'd a ſmall River which we took to be *Belus*, famous for its Sand, which is ſaid to be an excellent

cellent material for making Glaſs; as alſo to have miniſter'd the firſt occaſion and hint of that invention.

Here we began to decline from the Sea-Coaſt, upon which we had travelled ſo many days before, and to draw off more Eaſterly, croſſing obliquely over the Plain; and in two good hours we arriv'd at its farther ſide, where it is bounded by *Mount Carmel*. Here you find a narrow Valley letting you out of the Plain of *Acra* into that of *Eſdraelon*. Hereabouts is the end of the Tribe of *Aſher*, and the beginning of that of *Zabulon*; the borders of theſe two Tribes being thus deſcrib'd, *Joſh*.19. 26.

Paſſing thro' the narrow Valley which makes a communication between the two Plains, we arriv'd in two hours at that ancient River, the River *Kiſhon*; which cuts his way down the middle of the Plain of *Eſdraelon*, and then continuing his Courſe cloſe by the ſide of *Mount Carmel*, falls into the Sea, at a place called *Caypha*. In the condition we ſaw it, its Waters were low and inconſiderable: but in paſſing along the ſide of the Plain, we diſcern'd the tracks of many leſſer torrents, falling down into it from the Mountains; which muſt needs make it ſwell exceedingly upon ſudden Rains, as doubtleſs it actually did at the deſtruction of *Siſera*'s Hoſt, *Judg*.5.21. In three hours and a half from *Kiſhon* we came to a ſmall Brook, near which was an old Village and a good *Kane* call'd *Legune*: not far from which we took up our Quarters this Night. From this place we had a large proſpect of the Plain of *Eſdraelon*, which is of a vaſt extent, and very fertile, but uncultivated; only ſerving the Arabs for paſturage. At about ſix or ſeven hours diſtance Eaſtward ſtood within view *Nazareth*, and the two Mounts *Tabor* and *Hermon*. We were ſufficiently inſtructed by experience, what the holy *Pſalmiſt* means by *the Dew of Hermon*, our Tents being as wet with it, as if it had rain'd all Night. At about a Mile's diſtance from us was encamp'd *Chibly*, *Emir* of the Arabs, with his People and Cattle; and below upon the Brook *Kiſhon*, lay encamped another Clan of the Arabs, being the adverſe Party to *Chibly*. We had much the leſs satisfaction in this place, for being seated in the midst, between two such bad Neighbours. Our Stage this day was in all eight hours; our course South East by South, or thereabout.

Tuesday, Mar. 23.

Leaving this Lodging we arriv'd in one third of an hour at the *Emir*'s Tents, who came out in Person to take his Duties of us. We paid him * two Caphars, *viz.* one of *Lagune*, and another of *Jeneen*, and besides the Caphars, whatever else he was pleas'd to demand. He eased us in a very courteous manner of some of our Coats, which now (the heat both of the Climate and Season encreasing upon us) began to grow not only superfluous, but burdensom.

Getting quit of *Chibly* we turn'd out of the Plain of *Esdraelon*, and enter'd into the Precincts of the half Tribe of *Manasses*. From hence our Road lay for about four hours thro' narrow Valleys, pleasantly wooded on both sides. After which, crossing another small fruitful Plain, we came in half an hour to *Caphar Arab*, where we lodged. Our whole Stage exceeded not five hours; our Course being near as the day before.

Wednesday, Mar. 24.

Having paid our Caphar, we set out very early the next Morning; and leaving first *Arab*, and then *Rama* (two Mountain-Villages) on the right hand, we arriv'd in one hour at a fair Fountain called *Selee*, taking its Name from an adjacent Village. In one hour more we came to *Sebasta*. Here you leave the borders of the half Tribe of *Manasses*, and enter into those of the Tribe of *Ephraim*.

Sebasta is the Ancient *Samaria*, the Imperial City of the ten Tribes after their revolt from the House of *David*. It lost its former Name in the time of *Herod* the great, who rais'd it from a ruin'd to a most magnificent state, and called it, in honour of *Augustus Cæsar*, *Sebasta*. It is

* For both Caphars, eight *per* Frank, and three *per* Servant.

situate

situate upon a long Mount of an oval figure, having first a fruitful Valley, and then a ring of Hills running round about it. This great City is now wholly converted into Gardens; and all the tokens that remain, to testify that there has ever been such a place, are only, on the North side, a large square Piazza, encompass'd with Pillars, and on the East some poor remains of a great Church, said to have been built by the Empress *Helena*, over the place where St. *John Baptist* was both imprison'd and beheaded. In the Body of the Church you go down a Stair-case, into the very Dungeon, where that holy Blood was shed. The Turks (of whom here are a few poor Families) hold this Prison in great Veneration, and over it have erected a small Mosque; but for a little piece of money they suffer you to go in and satisfy your curiosity at pleasure.

Leaving *Sebasta* we pass'd in half an hour by *Sherack*, and in another half hour by *Barseba*, two Villages on the right hand; and then entring into a narrow Valley, lying East and West, and water'd with a fine Rivulet, we arrived in one hour at *Naplosa*.

Naplosa is the Ancient *Sychem*, or *Sychar*, as it is term'd in the New Testament. It stands in a narrow Valley between *Mount Gerizim* on the South, and *Ebal* on the North; being built at the foot of the former: For so the situation both of the City and Mountains is laid down by *Josephus*, *Antiq. Jud. Lib.* 5. *Cap.* 9. *Gerizim* (says he) hangeth over *Sychem*; and *Lib.* 4. *Cap. ult. Moses* commanded to erect an Altar toward the East, not far from *Sychem*, between *Mount Gerizim* on the right hand, (that is to one looking Eastward, on the South) and *Hebal* on the left (that is on the North:) Which so plainly assigns the position of these two Mountains, that it may be wonder'd, how Geographers should come to differ so much about it; or for what reason *Adrichomius* should place them both on the same side of the Valley of *Sychem*. From *Mount Gerizim* it was, that God commanded the Blessings to be pronounced upon the Children of *Israel*, and from *Mount Ebal* the Curses, *Deut.* 11. 29. Upon the former; the

Samaritans, whose chief residence is here at *Sychem*, have a small Temple or place of Worship, to which they are still wont to repair at certain seasons, for performance of the Rites of their Religion. What these Rites are I could not certainly learn: But that their Religion consists in the adoration of a Calf, as the Jews give out, seems to have more of spite than of truth in it.

Upon one of these Mountains also it was that God commanded the Children of *Israel* to set up great Stones, plaister'd over and inscrib'd with the Body of their Law; and to erect an Altar and to offer Sacrifices, feasting, and rejoycing before the Lord, *Deut.* 27. 4. But now whether *Gerizim* or *Ebal* was the place appointed for this Solemnity, there is some cause to doubt. The Hebrew Pentateuch, and ours from it, assigns *Mount Ebal* for this use; but the Samaritan asserts it to be *Gerizim*.

Our Company halting a little while at *Naplosa*, I had an opportunity to go and visit the Chief Priest of the Samaritans, in order to discourse with him, about this and some other difficulties occurring in the Pentateuch; which were recommended to me to be enquir'd about, by the learned Monsieur *Job Ludolphus*, Author of the Æthiopick History, when I visited him at *Franckford*, in my passage thro' *Germany*.

As for the difference between the Hebrew and Samaritan Copy, *Deut.* 27. 4. before cited; the Priest pretended the Jews had maliciously alter'd their Text, out of *odium* to the Samaritans; putting, for *Gerizim*, *Ebal*, upon no other account, but only because the Samaritans Worshipped in the former Mountain, which they would have, for that reason, not to be the true place appointed by God for his Worship and Sacrifice. To confirm this, he pleaded that *Ebal* was the Mountain of Cursing, *Deut.* 11. 29. and in its own nature an unpleasant place: but on the contrary *Gerizim* was the Mountain of Blessing by God's own appointment, and also in its self fertile and delightful; from whence he inferr'd a probability that this latter must have been the true Mountain, appointed for those

reli-

religious festivals, *Deut*. 27. 4. and not (as the Jews have corruptly written it) *Hebal*. We observ'd that to be, in some measure true which he pleaded concerning the nature of both Mountains: For tho' neither of the Mountains has much to boast of as to their pleasantness; yet as one passes between them, *Gerizim* seems to discover a somewhat more verdant fruitful aspect than *Ebal*. The reason of which may be, because fronting towards the North, it is shelter'd from the heat of the Sun by its own shade: Whereas *Ebal* looking Southward, and receiving the Sun that comes directly upon it, must by consequence be render'd more scorched and unfruitful. The Samaritan Priest could not say that any of those great Stones, which God directed *Joshua* to set up, were now to be seen in *Mount Gerizim*; which, were they now extant, would determine the question clearly on his side.

I enquir'd of him next what sort of Animal he thought those *Selavæ* might be, which the Children of *Israel* were so long fed with in the Wilderness, *Num*. 11. He answer'd, they were a sort of Fowls; and by the description, which he gave of them, I perceiv'd he meant the same kind with our Quails. I asked him what he thought of *Locusts*, and whether the History might not be better accounted for, supposing them to be the winged Creatures that fell so thick about the Camp of *Israel?* but by his answer, it appear'd, he had never heard of any such Hypothesis. Then I demanded of him, what sort of Plant or Fruit the *Dudaim*, or (as we translate it) *Mandrakes* were, which *Leah* gave to *Rachel*, for the purchase of her Husband's embraces? He said they were Plants of a large leaf, bearing a certain sort of Fruit, in shape resembling an Apple, growing ripe in Harvest, but of an ill savour, and not wholsome. But the virtue of them was to help Conception, being laid under the Genial Bed. That the Women were often wont so to apply it, at this day, out of an opinion of its prolifick virtue. Of these Plants I saw several afterwards in the way to *Jerusalem*; and if they were so common in *Mesopotamia*, as we saw them hereabout, one must

must either conclude that these could not be the true Mandrakes (*Dudaim,*) or else it would puzzle a good Critick to give a reason, why *Rachel* should purchase such vulgar things at so beloved and contested a price.

This Priest shew'd me a Copy of the Samaritan Pentateuch, but would not be perswaded to part with it upon any consideration. He had likewise the first Vol. of the English *Polyglot*, which he seem'd to esteem equally with his own Manuscript.

Naplosa is at present in a very mean condition, in comparison of what it is represented to have been anciently. It consists chiefly of two Streets lying parallel, under *Mount Gerizim*; but it is full of People, and the Seat of a *Bassa*.

Having paid our Caphar here, we set forward again in the Evening, and proceeding in the same narrow Valley, between *Gerizim* and *Ebal* (not above a furlong broad) we saw on our right hand just without the City, a small Mosque, said to have been built over the Sepulcher purchased by *Jacob*, of *Emmor* the Father of *Shechem*, *Gen.* 33. 19. It goes by the Name of *Joseph*'s Sepulcher, his bones having been here interr'd after their transportation out of *Egypt*, *Josh.* 24. 32.

At about one third of an hour from *Naplosa*, we came to *Jacob*'s *Well*; famous not only upon account of its Author, but much more for that memorable Conference, which our Blessed Saviour here had with the Woman of *Samaria*, *Joh.* 4. If it should be question'd whether this be the very Well that it is pretended for, or no; seeing it may be suspected to stand too remote from *Sychar*, for Women to come so far to draw Water? it is answer'd, that probably the City extended farther this way in former times than it does now; as may be conjectur'd from some pieces of a very thick Wall, still to be seen not far from hence. Over the Well there stood formerly a large Church, erected by that great and devout Patroness of the *Holy-Land*, the Empress *Helena*; but of this the voracity of time, assisted by the hands of the Turks, has

left

left nothing but a few Foundations remaining. The Well is cover'd at present with an old stone Vault, into which you are let down thro' a very strait hole; and then removing a broad flat stone, you discover the Mouth of the Well itself. It is dug in a firm Rock, and contains about three yards in diameter, and thirty five in depth; five of which, we found full of Water. This confutes a Story, commonly told to Travellers, who do not take the pains to examine the Well, *viz.* that it is dry all the Year round, except on the Anniversary of that Day on which our Blessed Saviour sat upon it; but then bubbles up with abundance of Water.

At this Well the narrow Valley of *Sychem* ends; opening it self into a wide Field, which is probably part of that parcel of ground, given by *Jacob* to his Son *Joseph*, *John.* 4. 5. It is water'd with a fresh Stream, rising between it and *Sychem*; which makes it so exceeding verdant and fruitful, that it may well be looked upon as a standing token of the tender affection of that good Patriarch to the best of Sons, *Gen.* 48. 22.

From *Jacob's Well* our Road went Southward, along a very spacious and fertile Valley. Having pass'd by two Villages on the right hand, one called *Howar*, the other *Sawee*; we arrived in four hours at *Kane Leban*, and lodged there. Our whole Stage to day was about eight hours; our Course variable between East and South.

Kane Leban stands on the East side of a delicious Vale, having a Village of the same Name standing opposite to it on the other side of the Vale. One of these places, either the *Kane* or the Village, is supposed to have been the *Lebonah* mentioned *Judg.* 11. 19. To which both the Name and Situation seem to agree.

Thursday, Mar. 25.

From *Kane Leban* our Road lay thro' a more Mountainous and rocky Country; of which we had a Specimen as soon as we were mounted the next Morning, our first task being to climb a very craggy and difficult Mountain.

tain. In three quarters of an hour we left, at ſome diſtance on the right hand, a Village call'd *Cinga*; and in one hour more, we entered into a very narrow Valley, between two high rocky hills, at the farther end of which we found the ruins of a Village, and of a Monaſtery. In this very place, or hereabouts, *Jacob's Bethel* is ſuppoſed to have been; where he had his ſtony Couch made eaſy by that beautifying viſion of God, and of the Angels aſcending, and deſcending, on a ladder reaching from Earth to Heaven, *Gen.* 28. Near this place are the Limits ſeparating between *Ephraim* and *Benjamin*, *Joſh.* 18. 13.

From hence we paſs'd thro' large Olive-yards; and having left, firſt *Geeb* and then *Selwid* (two Arab Villages) on the right hand, we came in an hour and a half to an old way cut with great labour over a rocky Precipice, and in one hour more we arriv'd at *Beer*. This is the place to which *Jotham* fled from the revenge of his Brother *Abimelech*, *Judg.* 9. 21. It is ſuppos'd alſo to be the ſame with *Michmas*, 1 *Sam.* 14.

Beer enjoys a very pleaſant ſituation, on an eaſy declivity fronting Southward. At the bottom of the Hill, it has a plentiful Fountain of excellent Water, from which it has its Name. At the upper ſide are remains of an old Church built by the Empreſs *Helena*, in memory of the Bleſſed Virgin, who when ſhe went in queſt of *the Child Jeſus*, as it is related, *Luke* 2.24. came (as tradition adds) to this City; and not finding Him whom her Soul loved, in the Company, ſhe ſat down weary and penſive at ſo ſad a diſappointment, in the very place where the Church now ſtands. But afterwards returning to *Jeruſalem*, ſhe had her maternal fears turned into joy, when *ſhe found Him ſitting in the Temple amongſt the Doctors, both hearing them, and asking them queſtions.*

All along this day's travel from *Kane Leban* to *Beer*, and alſo as far as we could ſee round, the Country diſcover'd quite a different face from what it had before; preſenting nothing to the view in moſt places, but naked

rocks,

rocks, mountains and precipices. At sight of which, Pilgrims are apt to be much astonished and baulked in their expectations; finding that Country in such an inhospitable condition, concerning whose pleasantness and plenty they had before form'd in their Minds such high Ideas from the description given of it, in the word of God: Insomuch that it almost startles their Faith, when they reflect, how it could be possible, for a land like this, to supply food for so prodigious a number of Inhabitants, as are said to have been polled in the twelve Tribes at one time; the sum given in by *Joab*, 2 *Sam.* 24. amounting to no less than thirteen hundred thousand fighting Men, besides Women and Children. But it is certain that any Man, who is not a little biass'd to Infidelity before, may see, as he passes along, arguments enough to support his Faith against such scruples.

For it is obvious for any one to observe, that these rocks and hills, must have been anciently cover'd with Earth, and cultivated, and made to contribute to the maintenance of the Inhabitants, no less than if the Country had been all plain: Nay perhaps much more; forasmuch as such a Mountainous and uneven surface affords a larger space of ground for cultivation, than this Country would amount to, if it were all reduced to a perfect level.

For the husbanding of these Mountains, their manner was to gather up the Stones, and place them in several lines, along the sides of the Hills, in form of a Wall. By such borders, they supported the mould from tumbling, or being wash'd down; and form'd many Beds of excellent Soil, rising gradually one above another, from the bottom to the top of the Mountains.

Of this form of culture you see evident footsteps, where-ever you go in all the Mountains of *Palestine*. Thus the very rocks were made fruitful. And perhaps there is no spot of ground in this whole land, that was not formerly improv'd, to the production of something or other, ministring to the sustenance of human life. For, than the plain Countries, nothing can be more fruitful, whether for the production of Corn or Cattle, and consequently of Milk. The Hills, tho' improper for all Cattle, except Goats, yet being disposed into such Beds as are afore describ'd, serv'd very well to bear Corn, Melons, Goards, Cucumbers, and such like Garden-stuff, which makes the principal food of these Countries for several Months in the Year. The most rocky parts of all, which could not well be adjusted in that manner for the production of Corn, might yet serve for the plantation of Vines and Olive Trees; which delight to extract, the one it's fatness, the other it's sprightly juice, chiefly out of such dry and flinty places. And the great Plain joyning to the dead Sea, which, by reason of its saltness, might be thought unserviceable both for Cattle, Corn, Olives and Vines, had yet its proper usefulness, for the nourishment of Bees, and for the fabrick of Honey; of which *Josephus* gives us his Testimony, *De Bell. Jud. Lib.* 5. *Cap.* 4. And I have reason to believe it, because when I was there, I perceiv'd in many places a smell of Honey and Wax, as strong as if one had been in an Apiary. Why then might not this Country very well maintain the vast number of its Inhabitants, being in every part so productive of either Milk, Corn, Wine, Oyl, or Honey, which are the principal food of these Eastern Nations? The constitution of their Bodies, and the nature of their Clime, enclining them to a more abstemious diet than we use in *England*, and other colder Regions. But I hasten to *Jerusalem*.

Leaving *Beer*, we proceeded as before, in a rude stony Country, which yet yielded us the sight of several old ruin'd Villages. In two hours and one third we came to the top of a Hill, from whence we had the first prospect of *Jerusalem*; *Rama* anciently call'd *Gibeah* of *Saul* being within view on the right hand, and the plain of *Jericho*, and the Mountains of *Gilead* on the left. In one hour more we approached the Walls of the holy City; but we could not enter immediately, it being necessary first to send a Messenger to acquaint the Governour of our arrival, and to desire liberty of entrance. Without which preceding

ceding Ceremony, no Frank dares come within the Walls. We therefore passed along by the West side of the City, and coming to the corner above *Bethlehem* Gate, made a stop there, in order to expect the return of our Messenger. We had not waited above half an hour, when he brought us our permission, and we enter'd accordingly at *Bethlehem* Gate. It is requir'd of all Franks, unless they happen to come in with some publick Minister, to dismount at the Gate, to deliver their arms, and enter on foot: But we coming in company with the French Consul, had the privilege to enter mounted and arm'd. Just within the Gate, we turned up a Street on the left hand, and were conducted by the Consul to his own house, with most friendly and generous invitations to make that our home, as long as we should continue at *Jerusalem.* Having taken a little refreshment, we went to the Latin Convent, at which all Frank Pilgrims are wont to be entertained. The Guardian and Friars received us with many kind welcomes; and kept us with them at Supper: After which we returned to the French Consul's to Bed. And thus we continued to take our Lodging at the Consul's, and our Board with the Friars, during our whole stay at *Jerusalem.*

Friday, March 26.

The next day being Good Friday in the Latin Style, the Consul was obliged to go into the Church of the Sepulcher, in order to keep his Feast; whither we accompanied him, altho' our own Easter was not till a week after theirs. We found the Church doors guarded by several *Janizaries,* and other Turkish Officers; who are plac'd here to watch, that none enter in, but such as have first paid their appointed Caphar. This is more or less according to the Country, or the Character of the Persons that enter. For Franks, it is ordinarily fourteen Dollars *per* head, unless they are Ecclesiasticks; for in that case it is but half so much.

Having once paid this Caphar, you may go in and out *gratis* as often as you please during the whole Feast; provided you take the ordinary opportunities, in which it is customary to open the doors: But if you would have them open'd at any time out of the common course, purposely for your own private occasion, then the first expence must be paid again.

The Pilgrims being all admitted this day, the Church doors were lock'd in the evening, and open'd no more till Easter day; by which we were kept in a close, but very happy confinement for three days. We spent our time in viewing the Ceremonies practis'd by the Latins at this Festival, and in visiting the several holy places; all which we had opportunity to survey, with as much freedom and deliberation as we pleased.

And now being got under the sacred Roof, and having the advantage of so much leisure and freedom, I might expatiate in a large description of the several holy places, which this Church (as a Cabinet) contains in it. But this would be a superfluous prolixity, so many Pilgrims having discharg'd this office with so much exactness already, and especially our learned sagacious Country-man Mr *Sandys*; whose descriptions and draughts, both of this Church, and also of the other remarkable places in and about *Jerusalem*, must be acknowledged so faithful and perfect, that they leave very little to be added by After-Comers, and nothing to be corrected. I shall content myself therefore, to relate only what pass'd in the Church during this Festival, saying no more of the Church it self, than just what is necessary to make my account intelligible.

The Church of the holy Sepulcher is founded upon *Mount Calvary*, which is a small Eminency or Hill upon the greater Mount of *Moriah*. It was anciently appropriated to the execution of Malefactors, and therefore shut out of the Walls of the City, as an execrable and polluted place. But since it was made the Altar on which was offer'd up the precious, and all-sufficient Sacrifice for the Sins of the whole World, it has recovered it self from that infamy, and has been always reverenc'd and resorted to, with such devotion by all Christians, that it has at-

tracted

UYT-LEGGINGE

Van de Tytel-plate.

Toren van den hoogen Choor.	A
Toren staende boven het Graf ons Heeren, met de ronde venster, door de welcke de Kercke haer meeste licht schept.	B
Den kostelijcken Klock-toren.	C
Toren van de Capelle, gebouwt op de plaetse daer de H. Maget stont, terwijlen haren Sone Jesus aen het kruys hingh.	D
Plaetse daer Abraham sijnen sone Isaac wilde op-offeren.	E
Plaetse daer Abraham den Ram sagh staen.	F
Gemetste Kerck-deure.	G
Kerck-deure gesloten ende gesegelt met den grooten Turcx segel, die de Officieren openen ende sluyten: waer in twee vier-kantige vensters zijn: door de een wordt de spijse ende den dranck in-gegeven voor de Natien die daer binnen woonen: door d'ander spreken die van buyten aen die van binnen zijn.	H
Het quartier der Griecken.	I
Het quartier der Abeyssinen.	K
De Minder-broeders onthalen de Pelgrims.	L
Turcksche Officieren, die de Kercke openen ende sluyten.	M
Den Vloer voor de Kercke schoon geplaveyt.	N
De punct van den Calvarien-bergh, daer het Kruys Christi is geplant geweest.	O
Steenen Trap, leydende van buyten tot op het top van den tooren van den hoogen Choor.	P

se uyt-legginge suldy in het langh beschreven vinden in het LXVII. Capittel des tweeden Boecks.

DEN GODTVRUGHTIGHEN PELGR
P
A
C
F
B
E
D
H
G
K
I
M
K
L
OFTE
IERUSALEMSCHE REYSE,
IN DRY BOECKEN BEDEYLT
Waer in veel ghedenckweerdighe saken verhaelt worde
midtsgaders eenighe gheestelycke Betrachtinghen
pass ende op de Mysterien van ieder heylige plaetse:
Alles ooghelijck bemerckt, ende bij een vergadert door den E.P. BER-
NARDINUS SURIUS, Minder-broeder Recollect. eertijdts COMMISSARIS
van het H. Landt, ende PRESIDENT van't H. Graf ons Heeren binnen
Ierusalem, in de jaren 1644. 45. 46. ende 47.
Vierden Druck met schoone Kopere Platen
Tot Brussel, by. IAN MOMNAERT, in de Druckerije. 1665.

tracted the City round about it, and ſtands now in the midſt of *Jeruſalem*, a great part of the Hill of *Sion* being ſhut out of the Walls, to make room for the admiſſion of *Calvary*.

In order to the fitting of this Hill for the Foundation of a Church, the firſt Founders were oblig'd to reduce it to a plain Area; which they did by cutting down ſeveral parts of the rock, and by elevating others. But in this work, care was taken, that none of thoſe parts of the Hill, which were reckon'd to be more immediately concern'd in our Bleſſed Lord's Paſſion, ſhould be alter'd or diminiſhed. Thus that very part of *Calvary*, where they ſay Chriſt was faſten'd to, and lifted upon his Croſs, is left entire; being about ten or twelve yards ſquare, and ſtanding at this day ſo high above the common floor of the Church, that you have 21 ſteps or ſtairs to go up to its top: And the holy Sepulcher it ſelf, which was at firſt a Cave hewn into the rock under ground, having had the rock cut away from it all round, is now as it were a Grotto above ground.

The Church is leſs than one hundred paces long, and not more than ſixty wide: and yet is ſo contriv'd, that it is ſuppoſed to contain under its Roof twelve or thirteen Sanctuaries, or places conſecrated to a more than ordinary veneration, by being reputed to have ſome particular actions done in them, relating to the Death and Reſurrection of Chriſt. As firſt, the place where he was derided by the Souldiers: ſecondly, where the Souldiers divided his Garments: thirdly, where he was ſhut up, whilſt they digg'd the hole to ſet the foot of the Croſs in, and made all ready for his Crucifixion: fourthly, where he was nailed to the Croſs: fifthly, where the Croſs was erected: ſixthly, where the Souldier ſtood, that pierced his ſide: ſeventhly, where his Body was anointed in order to his Burial: eighthly, where his Body was depoſited in the Sepulcher: ninthly, where the Angels appear'd to the Women after his Reſurrection: tenthly, where Chriſt Himſelf appear'd to *Mary Magdalen*, &c. The places where theſe

these and many other things relating to our Bleſſed Lord are ſaid to have been done, are all ſuppos'd to be contain'd within the narrow precincts of this Church, and are all diſtinguiſhed and adorned with ſo many ſeveral Altars.

In Galleries round about the Church, and alſo in little Buildings annext to it on the out ſide, are certain apartments for the reception of Fryars and Pilgrims; and in theſe places almoſt every Chriſtian Nation anciently maintain'd a ſmall Society of Monks; each Society having its proper quarter aſſign'd to it, by the appointment of the Turks: Such as the Latins, Greeks, Syrians, Armenians, Abyſſines, Georgians, Neſtorians, Cophtites, Maronites, *&c.* all which had anciently their ſeveral apartments in the Church. But theſe have all, except four, forſaken their Quarters; not being able to ſuſtain the ſevere rents and extortions, which their Turkiſh Landlords impoſe upon them. The Latins, Greeks, Armenians and Cophtites keep their footing ſtill, but of theſe four, the Cophtites have now only one poor repreſentative of their Nation left: And the Armenians are run ſo much in debt, that 'tis ſuppoſed they are haſtning apace to follow the examples of their Brethren, who have deſerted before them.

Beſides their ſeveral apartments, each Fraternity have their Altars and Sanctuary, properly and diſtinctly allotted to their own uſe. At which places they have a peculiar right to perform their own Divine Service, and to exclude other Nations from them.

But that which has always been the great prize contended for by the ſeveral Sects, is the command and appropriation of the holy Sepulcher: A privilege conteſted with ſo much unchriſtian fury and animoſity, eſpecially between the Greeks and Latins, that in diſputing which Party ſhould go into it to celebrate their Maſs, they have ſometimes proceeded to blows and wounds even at the very door of the Sepulcher; mingling their own blood with their Sacrifices. An evidence of which Fury the Father Guardian ſhewed us in a great ſcar upon his Arm, which he told us was the mark of a wound given him

by

by a sturdy Greek Priest in one of these unholy Wars. Who can expect ever to see these holy places rescued from the hands of Infidels? Or if they should be recover'd, what deplorable contests might be expected to follow about them? seeing even in their present State of Captivity, they are made the occasion of such unchristian rage and animosity.

For putting an end to these infamous Quarrels, the French King interpos'd, by a Letter to the Grand Visier about twelve years since; requesting him to order the holy Sepulcher to be put into the hands of the Latins, according to the tenour of the Capitulation made in the year *1673*. The consequence of which Letter, and of other instances made by the French King, was, that the holy Sepulcher was appropriated to the Latins: This was not accomplish'd till the year *1690*, they alone having the privilege to say Mass in it. And tho' it be permitted to Christians of all Nations to go into it for their private devotions, yet none may solemnize any publick office of Religion there, but the Latins.

The dayly employment of these Recluses is to trim the Lamps, and to make devotional visits and processions to the several Sanctuaries in the Church. Thus they spend their time, many of them for four or six years together: Nay so far are some transported with the pleasing contemplations in which they here entertain themselves, that they will never come out to their dying day, burying themselves (as it were) alive in our Lord's Grave.

The Latins, of whom there are always about ten or twelve residing at the Church, with a President over them, make every day a solemn procession, with Tapers and Crucifixes, and other processionary solemnities, to the several Sanctuaries; singing at every one of them a Latin Hymn relating to the subject of each place. These Latins being more polite and exact in their functions than the other Monks here residing, and also our conversation being chiefly with them, I will only describe their Ceremonies, without taking notice of what was done by others,

others, who did not ſo much come under our obſervation.

Their Ceremony begins on Good Friday night, which is call'd by them the *Nox tenebroſa*, and is obſerv'd with ſuch an extraordinary ſolemnity, that I cannot omit to give a particular deſcription of it.

As ſoon as it grew dusk, all the Fryars and Pilgrims were conven'd in the Chappel of the Apparition (which is a ſmall Oratory on the North ſide of the Holy Grave, adjoyning to the apartments of the Latins) in order to go in a proceſſion round the Church. But, before they ſet out, one of the Fryars Preached a Sermon in Italian in that Chappel. He began his diſcourſe thus; *In queſta notte tenebroſa, &c.* at which words all the Candles were inſtantly put out, to yield a livelier Image of the occaſion. And ſo we were held by the Preacher, for near half an hour, very much in the dark. Sermon being ended, every Perſon preſent had a large lighted Taper put into his hand, as if it were to make amends for the former darkneſs; and the Crucifixes and other Utenſils were diſpos'd in order for beginning the proceſſion. Amongſt the other Crucifixes, there was one of a very large ſize, which bore upon it the Image of our Lord, as big as the Life. The Image was faſten'd to it with great nails, Crown'd with Thorns, beſmear'd with Blood; and ſo exquiſitely was it form'd, that it repreſented in a very lively manner the lamentable ſpectacle of our Lord's Body, as it hung upon the Croſs. This Figure was carried all along in the head of the proceſſion; after which, the Company follow'd to all the Sanctuaries in the Church, ſinging their appointed Hymn at every one.

The firſt place they viſited was that of the Pillar of Flagellation, a large piece of which is kept in a little Cell juſt at the door of the Chappel of the Apparition. There they ſung their proper Hymn; and another Fryar entertain'd the Company with a Sermon in Spaniſh, touching the ſcourging of our Lord.

From

Uyt-legghinghe van den Bergh Calvarie.

A. d'Eerste Capelle van den bergh Calvarie.
B. De tweede Capelle.
C. De scheure in de steen-rotse.
D. De scheure continuerende in de Capelle benedẽ daer Adams hooft ghevonden wierdt.
E. Het Graf van Godefridus de Boüillon.
F. Het Graf syns Broeders Baldewyn de Boüillon.
G. Den steen der Salvinge.
H. Den op-gangh tot den Berg van Calvarien.
I. Den neder-gangh tot de plaetse van de vindinge des H Kruys.
K. De Kerck-deure die nu toe-gemetst is.
L. De groote Kerck-deure door de welke men in de Kercke gaet, als men kan sien in de tytel-plate, in 't beginsel van den Boeck.

Vytlegginghe van het H. Graf onses Salighmakers.

A. Den Copolo oft Cap van het H. Graf.
B. Het H. Graf.
C. De Galerye.
D. Den Autaer van binnen.
E. 't Binnenste des Portaels.
F. Den ingangh des Portaels.
G. Den in-gangh van h Graf.
H. Den steen daer den E gel op geseten heeft

From hence they proceeded in ſolemn order to the Priſon of Chriſt, where they pretend he was ſecur'd whilſt the Souldiers made things ready for his Crucifixion; here likewiſe they ſung their Hymn, and a third Fryar preach'd in French.

From the Priſon they went to the Altar of the diviſion of Chriſt's Garments; where they only ſung their Hymn, without adding any Sermon.

Having done here, they advanced to the Chappel of the Deriſion; at which, after their Hymn, they had a fourth Sermon (as I remember) in French.

From this place they went up to *Calvary*, leaving their Shoes at the bottom of the Stairs. Here are two Altars to be viſited: One where our Lord is ſuppoſed to have been nail'd to his Croſs; Another where his Croſs was erected. At the former of theſe they laid down the great Crucifix, (which I but now deſcribed) upon the Floor, and acted a kind of a reſemblance of Chriſt's being nailed to the Croſs; and after the Hymn, one of the Fryars preached another Sermon in Spaniſh, upon the Crucifixion.

From hence they remov'd to the adjoyning Altar, where the Croſs is ſuppoſed to have been erected, bearing the Image of our Lord's Body. At this Altar is a hole in the natural Rock, ſaid to be the very ſame individual one, in which the foot of our Lord's Croſs ſtood. Here they ſet up their Croſs, with the bloody Crucified Image upon it; and leaving it in that poſture, they firſt ſung their Hymn, and then the Father Guardian, ſitting in a Chair before it, preached a Paſſion Sermon in Italian.

At about one yard and a half diſtance from the hole in which the foot of the Croſs was fix'd, is ſeen that memorable cleft in the Rock, ſaid to have been made by the Earthquake which happen'd at the ſuffering of the God of Nature; When (as St *Matthew*, *Chap.* 27. *v.* 51. witneſſeth) *the rocks rent, and the very graves were opened.* This cleft, as to what now appears of it, is about a ſpan wide at its upper part, and two deep; after which it cloſes: but it opens again below, (as you may ſee in another

Chappel contiguous to the side of *Calvary* ;) and runs down to an unknown depth in the Earth. That this rent was made by the Earthquake, that happened at our Lord's Passion; there is only tradition to prove: But that it is a natural and genuine breach, and not counterfeited by any Art, the sense and reason of every one that sees it may convince him ; for the sides of it fit like two Tallys to each other ; and yet it runs in such intricate windings as could not well be counterfeited by Art, nor arriv'd at by any Instruments.

The Ceremony of the Passion being over, and the Guardian's Sermon ended, two Fryars, personating the one *Joseph* of *Arimathea*, the other *Nicodemus*, approach'd the Cross, and with a most solemn concern'd air, both of aspect and behaviour, drew out the great Nails, and took down the feigned Body from the Cross. It was an Effigies so contriv'd, that its Limbs were soft and flexible, as if they had been real Flesh : and nothing could be more surprising, than to see the two pretended Mourners bend down the Arms, which were before extended, and dispose them upon the Trunk, in such a manner as is usual in Corpses.

The Body being taken down from the Cross, was receiv'd in a fair large winding-sheet, and carried down from *Calvary* ; the whole Company attending as before, to the Stone of Unction. This is taken for the very place where the precious Body of our Lord was anointed, and prepared for the Burial, *John.* 19. 39. Here they laid down their imaginary Corps ; and casting over it several sweet Powders and Spices, wrapt it up in the winding-sheet : Whilst this was doing, they sung their proper Hymn, and afterwards one of the Fryars preached in Arabick, a Funeral Sermon.

These Obsequies being finished, they carried off their fancied Corps, and laid it in the Sepulcher ; shutting up the door till Easter morning. And now after so many Sermons, and so long, not to say tedious a Ceremony, it may well be imagined, that the weariness of the Congregation, as well as the hour of the night, made it needful to go to rest.

Satur-

Saturday, *Mar*. 27.

The next morning nothing extraordinary paſs'd; which gave many of the Pilgrims leiſure to have their Arms mark'd with the uſual enſigns of *Jeruſalem*. The Artiſts, who undertake the operation, do it in this manner. They have ſtamps in Wood of any figure that you deſire; which they firſt print off upon your Arm with powder of Charcoal: Then taking two very fine Needles ty'd cloſe together, and dipping them often, like a Pen, in certain Ink, compounded as I was informed of Gunpowder and Ox-Gall, they make with them ſmall punctures all along the lines of the figure which they have printed; and then waſhing the part in wine, conclude the work. Theſe punctures they make with great quickneſs and dexterity, and with ſcarce any ſmart, ſeldom piercing ſo deep as to draw Blood.

In the Afternoon of this day, the Congregation was aſſembled in the Area before the Holy Grave; where the Fryars ſpent ſome hours in ſinging over the Lamentations of *Jeremiah*; which Function, with the uſual proceſſion to the holy places, was all the Ceremony of this day.

Sunday, *Mar*. 28.

On Eaſter morning, the Sepulcher was again ſet open very early. The Clouds of the former morning were clear'd up; and the Fryars put on a face of joy and ſerenity, as if it had been the real juncture of our Lord's Reſurrection. Nor doubtleſs was this joy feigned, whatever their mourning might be; this being the day in which their Lenten diſciplines expir'd, and they were come to a full belly again.

The Maſs was celebrated this morning juſt before the Holy Sepulcher, being the moſt eminent place in the Church; where the Father Guardian had a Throne erected, and being array'd in Epiſcopal Robes, with a Mitre on his Head, in the ſight of the Turks, he gave the Hoſt to all that were diſpos'd to receive it; not refuſing Children of ſeven or eight years old. This office being ended, we made our exit out of the Sepulcher, and returning to the Convent, din'd with the Fryars.

After dinner, we took an opportunity to go and viſit ſome of the remarkable places without the City Walls; We began with thoſe on the North ſide.

The firſt place we were conducted to was a large Grot, a little without *Damaſcus* Gate; ſaid to have been ſome time the reſidence of *Jeremiah*. On the left ſide of it, is ſhewn the Prophet's Bed, being a ſhelve on the Rock, about eight foot from the ground; and not far from this, is the place where they ſay he wrote his Lamentations. This place is at preſent a College of Derviſes, and is held in great veneration by the Turks and Jews, as well as Chriſtians.

The next place we came to was thoſe famous Grots call'd the Sepulchers of the Kings; but for what reaſon they go by that Name is hard to reſolve: For it is certain none of the Kings, either of *Iſrael* or *Judah*, were buried here; the holy Scriptures aſſigning other places for their Sepultures; unleſs it may be thought perhaps that *Hezekiah* was here interr'd, and that theſe were the Sepulchers of the Sons of *David*, mention'd 2 *Chron*. 32. 33. Whoever was buried here, this is certain, that the place it ſelf diſcovers ſo great an expence both of labour and treaſure, that we may well ſuppoſe it to have been the work of Kings. You approach to it at the Eaſt ſide, thro' an entrance cut out of the natural Rock, which admits you into an open Court of about forty paces ſquare, cut down into the Rock, with which it is encompaſs'd inſtead of Walls. On the South ſide of the Court, is a Portico nine paces long and four broad, hewn likewiſe out of the natural Rock. This is a kind of Architrave running along its front, adorn'd with Sculpture of fruits and flowers, ſtill diſcernible, but by time much defac'd. At the end of the Portico on the left hand, you deſcend to the paſſage into the Sepulchers. The door is now ſo obſtructed with

ſtones

ſtones and rubbiſh, that it is a thing of ſome difficulty to creep thro' it. But within, you arrive in a large fair Room, about ſeven or eight yards ſquare, cut out of the natural Rock. Its ſides and Ceiling are ſo exactly ſquare, and its Angles ſo juſt, that no Architect with Levels and Plummets could build a Room more regular: And the whole is ſo firm and entire, that it may be call'd a Chamber hollow'd out of one piece of Marble. From this Room, you paſs into (I think) ſix more, one within another, all of the ſame Fabrick with the firſt. Of theſe, the two innermoſt are deeper than the reſt, having a ſecond deſcent of about ſix or ſeven ſteps into them.

In every one of theſe Rooms except the firſt, were Coffins of ſtone plac'd in Niches in the ſides of the Chambers. They had been at firſt cover'd with handſome lids, and carv'd with Garlands; but now moſt of them were broke to pieces by ſacrilegious hands. The ſides and Ceiling of the Rooms were always dropping, with the moiſt damps condenſing upon them. To remedy which nuiſance, and to preſerve theſe Chambers of the dead, polite and clean, there was in each Room a ſmall channel cut in the floor, which ſerv'd to drain the drops that fall conſtantly into it.

But the moſt ſurpriſing thing belonging to theſe ſubterraneous Chambers was their doors; of which there is only one that remains hanging, being left as it were on purpoſe to puzzle the beholders. It conſiſted of a plank of Stone of about ſix inches in thickneſs, and in its other dimenſions equalling the ſize of an ordinary door, or ſomewhat leſs. It was carv'd in ſuch a manner, as to reſemble a piece of wainſcot: The Stone of which it was made was viſibly of the ſame kind with the whole Rock; and it turn'd upon two hinges in the nature of Axels, as is repreſented in the marginal figure. Theſe hinges were of the ſame entire piece of ſtone with the door; and were

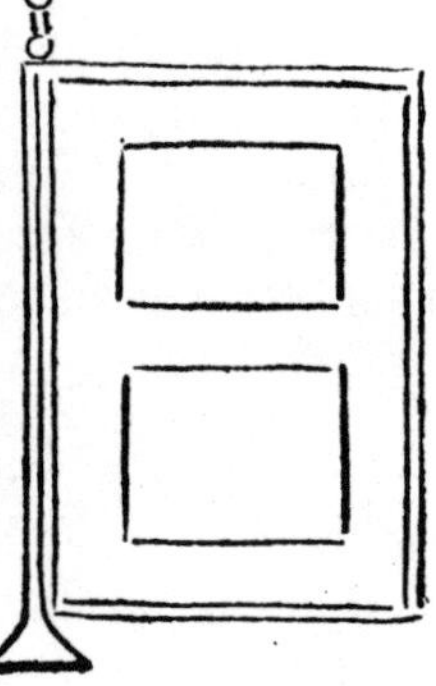

contain'd

contain'd in two holes of the immoveable Rock, one at the top, the other at the bottom.

From this description it is obvious to start a question, how such doors as these were made; whether they were cut out of the Rock, in the same place and manner as they now hang; or whether they were brought, and fix'd in their station like other doors? One of these must be suppos'd to have been done; and which soever part we choose, as most probable, it seems at first glance to be not without its difficulty. But thus much I have to say, for the resolving of this riddle (which is wont to create no small dispute amongst Pilgrims) *viz.* That the door which was left hanging, did not touch its lintel, by at least two inches; so that I believe it might easily have been lifted up, and unhinged. And the doors which had been thrown down, had their hinges at the upper end, twice as long as those at the bottom; which seems to intimate pretty plainly, by what method this work was accomplished.

From these Sepulchers, we return'd toward the City again, and just by *Herod*'s Gate were shewn a Grotto full of filthy Water and Mire. This passes for the Dungeon in which *Jeremiah* was kept by *Zedekiah*, till enlarged by the Charity of *Ebed Melech, Jer.* 38. At this place we concluded our visits for that evening.

Monday, Mar. 29.

The next day being Easter Monday, the Mosolem or Governour of the City set out, according to custom, with several Bands of Souldiers to convey the Pilgrims to *Jordan.* Without this guard, there is no going thither, by reason of the Multitude and Insolence of the Arabs in these parts. The fee to the Mosolem for his Company and Souldiers upon this occasion, is twelve Dollars for each Frank Pilgrim, but if they be Ecclesiasticks, six; which you must pay, whether you are dispos'd to go the Journey or stay in the City. We went out at St *Stephen*'s Gate, being in all, of every Nation and Sex, about two thousand Pilgrims. Having cross'd the Valley of *Jehosaphat,*

Vyt legginghe van de Vlecke Bethania.

A. Den Olyf-bergh.
B. Bethphage.
C. De fonteyne der Apostelen.
D. Daer het huys van Martha stondt.
E. Den steen daer Christus op sat.
F. Daer het huys van Magdalena ghestaen heeft.
G. Het Graf van Lazarus.
H. Het huys van Lazarus.
I. Het huys van Simon den Melaetschen.
K. Het dal van den vervloekten vyge-boom.
L. Den wegh naer Jerusalem.
M. Den Jordan.

ſaphat, and part of *Mount Olivet*, we came in half an hour to *Bethany*; at preſent only a ſmall Village. At the firſt entrance into it, is an old ruin, which they call *Lazarus*'s Caſtle, ſuppoſed to have been the Manſion Houſe of that favourite of our Lord. At the bottom of a ſmall deſcent, not far from the Caſtle, is ſhewn the Sepulcher out of which he was rais'd to a ſecond Mortality, by that enlivening voice of Chriſt, *Lazarus come forth*. You deſcend into the Sepulcher by twenty five ſteep Stairs; at the bottom of which, you arrive firſt in a ſmall ſquare Room, and from thence you creep down into another leſſer Room about a yard and a half deeper, in which the Body is ſaid to have been laid. This place is held in great veneration by the Turks, who uſe it for an Oratory, and demand of all Chriſtians a ſmall Caphar for their admiſſion into it.

About a Bow ſhot from hence you paſs by the place which, they ſay, was *Mary Magdalen*'s Habitation; and then deſcending a ſteep Hill, you come to the Fountain of the *Apoſtles*; ſo call'd becauſe, as the tradition goes, thoſe holy Perſons were wont to refreſh themſelves here, in their frequent Travels between *Jeruſalem* and *Jericho*. And indeed it is a thing very probable, and no more than I believe is done by all that travel this way; the Fountain being cloſe by the Road ſide, and very inviting to the thirſty Paſſenger.

From this place you proceed in an intricate way amongſt Hills and Valleys interchangeably; all of a very barren aſpect at preſent, but diſcovering evident ſigns of the labour of the Husband-man in ancient times. After ſome hours travel in this ſort of road, you arrive at the Mountainous Deſart into which our Bleſſed Saviour was led by the Spirit, to be tempted by the Devil. A moſt miſerable dry barren place it is, conſiſting of high rocky Mountains, ſo torn and diſorder'd, as if the Earth had here ſuffer'd ſome great convulſion, in which its very bowels had been turn'd outward. On the left hand looking down in a deep Valley, as we paſſed along, we ſaw ſome ruins of ſmall Cells and Cottages; which they told us were formerly ly the Habitations of Hermits retiring hither for Penance and Mortification. And certainly there could not be found in the whole Earth a more comfortless and abandon'd place, for that purpose. From the top of these Hills of desolation, we had however a delightful prospect of the Mountains of *Arabia*, the *Dead Sea* and the Plain of *Jericho*; into which last place we descended, after about five hours March from *Jerusalem*. As soon as we entered the Plain, we turn'd up on the left hand, and going about one hour that way, came to the foot of the *Quarantania*; which, they say, is the Mountain into which the Devil took our Blessed Saviour, when he tempted him with that visionary scene of all the Kingdoms and Glories of the World. It is, as St *Matthew* styles it, an exceeding high Mountain, and in its ascent not only difficult, but dangerous. It has a small Chappel at the top, and another about half way up, founded upon a Prominent part of the rock: near this latter are several Caves and holes in the side of the Mountain, made use of anciently by Hermits, and by some at this day, for places to keep their Lent in; in imitation of that of our Blessed Saviour. In most of these Grots we found certain Arabs quarter'd with Fire-Arms, who obstructed our ascent, demanding two hundred Dollars for leave to go up the Mountains. So we departed without farther trouble, not a little glad to have so good an excuse for not climbing so dangerous a Precipice.

Turning down from hence into the Plain, we pass'd by a ruin'd Aqueduct, and a Convent in the same condition: And in about a miles riding came to the Fountain of *Elisha*; so call'd, because miraculously purg'd from its brackishness by that Prophet, at the request of the Men of *Jericho*, 2 *Kings* 2. 19. Its Waters are at present receiv'd in a Basin, about nine or ten paces long, and five or six broad; and from thence issuing out in good plenty, divide themselves into several small streams, dispersing their refreshment to all the Field between this and *Jericho*, and rendring it exceeding fruitful. Close by the Fountain grows a large Tree spreading into Boughs over the Water,

and

and here in the ſhade we took a Collation, with the Father Guardian, and about thirty or forty Fryars more, who went this Journey with us.

At about one third of an hours diſtance from hence is *Jericho*, at preſent only a poor naſty Village of the Arabs. We were here carried to ſee a place where *Zaccheus*'s Houſe is ſaid to have ſtood; which is only an old ſquare ſtone building, on the South ſide of *Jericho*. About two furlongs from hence, the Moſolem, with his People had encamp'd; and not far from them we took up our Quarters this night.

Tueſday, Mar. 30.

The next morning we ſet out very early for *Jordan*, where we arriv'd in two hours. We found the Plain very barren as we paſs'd along it, producing nothing but a kind of Samphire, and other ſuch marine Plants. I obſerv'd in many places of the road, where puddles of water had ſtood, a whiteneſs upon the ſurface of the ground; which, upon tryal, I found to be a cruſt of Salt caus'd by the water to riſe out of the Earth, in the ſame manner as it does every year in the Valley of Salt near *Aleppo*, after the Winter's Inundation. Theſe Saline efflореſcencies I found at ſome leagues diſtance from the *Dead Sea*; which demonſtrates, that the whole Valley muſt be all over plentifully impregnated with that Mineral.

Within about a furlong of the river, at that place where we viſited it, there was an old ruin'd Church and Convent, dedicated to St *John* in memory of the Baptizing of our Bleſſed Lord. It is founded as near as could be conjectur'd to the very place where he had the honour to perform that ſacred office, and to waſh Him who was infinitely purer than the Water it ſelf. On the farther ſide of the foremention'd Convent there runs along a ſmall deſcent, which you may fitly call the firſt and outermoſt bank of *Jordan*; as far as which it may be ſuppos'd the river does, or at leaſt did anciently overflow, at ſome Seaſons of the Year, *viz.* at the time of Harveſt, *Joſh.* 3.15.

L or

or as it is expreſs'd, *Chron.* 12. 15. in the firſt Month, that is, in *March*. But at preſent (whether it be becauſe the River has, by its rapidity of current, worn its Channel deeper than it was formerly, or whether becauſe its Waters are diverted ſome other way) it ſeems to have forgot its ancient greatneſs: For we could diſcern no ſign or probability of ſuch overflowings, when we were there; which was the thirtieth of *March*, being the proper time for theſe Inundations. Nay ſo far was the River from overflowing, that it ran at leaſt two yards below the brink of its Channel.

After having deſcended the outermoſt bank, you go about a furlong upon a level ſtrand, before you come to the immediate bank of the river. This ſecond bank is ſo beſet with Buſhes and Trees, ſuch as Tamarisk, Willows, Oleanders, *&c.* that you can ſee no Water till you have made your way thro' them. In this thicket anciently (and the ſame is reported of it at this day) ſeveral ſorts of wild Beaſts were wont to harbour themſelves. Whoſe being waſhed out of the Covert by the overflowings of the river, gave occaſion to that alluſion, *Jerem.* 49. 19. and 50. 44. *He ſhall come up like a lion from the ſwelling of Jordan.*

No ſooner were we arriv'd at the river, and diſmounted, in order to ſatisfy that curioſity and devotion, which brought us thither, but we were alarm'd by ſome Troops of Arabs appearing on the other ſide, and firing at us; but at too great a diſtance to do any execution. This intervening diſturbance hindred the Fryars from performing their ſervice preſcrib'd for this place; and ſeem'd to put them in a terrible fear of their lives, beyond what appear'd in the reſt of the Company: Tho' conſidering the ſordidneſs of their preſent condition, and the extraordinary rewards, which they boaſt to be their due in the World to come, one would think in reaſon, they of all Men ſhould have the leaſt cauſe to diſcover ſo great a fear of Death, and ſo much fondneſs of a life like theirs.

But

But this Alarm was ſoon over, and every one return'd to his former purpoſe: ſome ſtripp'd and bath'd themſelves in the River; others cut down boughs from the Trees; every Man was employ'd one way or other to take a memorial of this famous Stream. The Water was very turbid, and two rapid to be ſwam againſt. For its breadth, it might be about twenty yards over; and in depth it far exceeded my height. On the other ſide there ſeem'd to be a much larger thicket than on that where we were: But we durſt not ſwim over, to take any certain account of that Region, for fear of the Arabs; there being three Guns fired juſt over againſt us, and (as we might gueſs by their reports) very near the river.

Having finiſhed our deſign here, we were ſummon'd to return, by the Moſolem; who carried us back into the middle of the Plain, and there ſitting under his Tent, made us paſs before him, Man by Man, to the end he might take the more exact account of us, and loſe nothing of his Caphar. We ſeem'd at this place to be near the *Dead Sea*, and ſome of us had a great deſire to go nearer, and take a view of thoſe prodigious Waters. But this could not be attempted, without the Licence of our Commander in chief. We therefore ſent to requeſt his permiſſion for our going, and a guard to attend us; both which he readily granted, and we immediately proſecuted our purpoſe.

Coming within about half an hour of the Sea, we found the ground uneven, and varied into hillocks, much reſembling thoſe places in *England* where there have been anciently Lime-kilns. Whether theſe might be the Pits at which the Kings of *Sodom and Gomorrah* were overthrown by the four Kings, *Gen*. 14. 10. I will not determine.

Coming near the Sea we paſs'd thro' a kind of Coppice, of Buſhes and Reeds; In the midſt of which our Guide, who was an Arab, ſhew'd us a Fountain of freſh Water, riſing not above a furlong from the Sea: Freſh Water he call'd it, but we found it brackiſh.

The *Dead Sea* is encloſ'd on the Eaſt and Weſt with exceeding high Mountains; on the North it is bounded with the Plain of *Jericho*, on which side also it receives the Waters of *Jordan*; On the South it is open, and extends beyond the reach of the Eye. It is said to be twenty four leagues long, and six or seven broad.

On the shore of the Lake we found a black sort of Pebbles, which being held in the flame of a Candle soon burns, and yields a smoak of an intolerable stench. It has this property, that it loses only of its weight, but not of its bulk by burning. The hills bordering upon the Lake, are said to abound with this sort of Sulphureous Stones. I saw pieces of it, at the Convent of St *John* in the Wilderness, two foot square. They were carved in Basso Relievo, and polish'd to as great a lustre as black Marble is capable of, and were design'd for the ornament of the new Church at the Convent.

It is a common tradition, that Birds, attempting to fly over this Sea, drop down dead into it; and that no Fish, nor other sort of Animal can endure these deadly Waters. The former report I saw actually confuted, by several Birds flying about and over the Sea, without any visible harm: The latter also I have some reason to suspect as false, having observed amongst the Pebbles on the shore, two or three shells of Fish resembling Oyster-shells. These were cast up by the Waves, at two hours distance from the Mouth of *Jordan*: Which I mention, lest it should be suspected that they might be brought into the Sea that way.

As for the Bitumen, for which the Sea had been so famous, there was none at the place where we were. But it is gather'd near the Mountains on both sides in great plenty. I had several lumps of it brought me to *Jerusalem*. It exactly resembles Pitch, and cannot readily be distinguish'd from it, but by the Sulphureousness of its Smell and Taste.

The Water of the Lake was very limpid, and salt to the highest degree; and not only salt, but also extream bitter and nauseous. Being willing to make an experiment of its strength, I went into it, and found it bore up my my Body in ſwimming with an uncommon force. But as for that relation of ſome Authors, that Men wading into it were buoyed up to the top, as ſoon as they go as deep as the Navel; I found it, upon experiment, not true.

Being deſirous to ſee the remains (if there were any) of thoſe Cities anciently ſituate in this place; and made ſo dreadful an example of the divine vengeance, I diligently ſurvey'd the waters, as far as my Eye could reach: But neither could I diſcern any heaps of ruins, nor any ſmoak aſcending above the ſurface of the water; as is uſually deſcribed in the writings and maps of Geographers. But yet I muſt not omit what was confidently atteſted to me by the Father Guardian, and Procurator of *Jeruſalem*; both Men in years, and ſeemingly not deſtitute either of ſenſe or probity: *viz.* that they had once actually ſeen one of theſe ruins; that it was ſo near the ſhore, and the waters ſo ſhallow, at that time, that they together with ſome French Men went to it, and found there ſeveral Pillars, and other fragments of Buildings. The cauſe of our being depriv'd of this ſight was, I ſuppoſe, the height of the water.

On the Weſt ſide of the Sea is a ſmall Promontory, near which, as our Guides told us, ſtood the Monument of *Lot*'s Metamorphos'd Wife; part of which (if they may be credited) is viſible at this day. But neither would the preſent occaſion permit us to go and examine the truth of this relation; neither, had the opportunity ſerv'd, could we give faith enough to their report, to induce us to go on ſuch an errand.

As for the Apples of *Sodom* ſo much talk'd of, I neither ſaw, nor heard of any hereabouts: Nor was there any Tree to be ſeen near the Lake, from which one might expect ſuch a kind of Fruit; * which induces me to believe that there may be a greater deceit in this Fruit, than that which is uſually reported of it; and that its very being, as well as its beauty is a fiction, only kept up, as my Lord *Bacon* obſerves many other falſe notions are,

* *Tacit. Hiſt. Lib. 5. Joſeph. Bell. Jud. Lib. 5. Cap. 5.*

because

becauſe it ſerves for a good alluſion, and helps the Poets to a Similitude.

In our return from the *Dead Sea*, at about one hours diſtance from it, we came to an old ruin'd Greek Convent. There was good part of the Church remaining, with ſeveral pieces of painting entire; as the figures of ſeveral Greek Saints, and over the Altar the repreſentation of our Lord's laſt Supper, with this Text of holy Writ fairly inſcrib'd, Λάβετε φάγετε, &c. Hereabout, and alſo in many other places of the Plain, I perceiv'd a ſtrong ſcent of Honey and Wax, (the Sun being very hot;) and the Bees were very induſtrious about the bloſſoms of that ſalt weed which the Plain produces. In about one hour and a half more we returned to our Tents and Company, at the ſame place where we ſlept the night before; and there we ſpent this night alſo.

Amongſt the products of this place, I ſaw a very remarkable Fruit call'd by the Arabs *Za-cho-ne*. It grows upon a thorny Buſh, with ſmall Leaves; and both in ſhape and colour reſembles a ſmall unripe Wallnut. The kernels of this Fruit the Arabs bray in a Mortar; and then putting the pulp into ſcalding water, they skim off an Oyl, which riſes to the top. This Oyl they take inwardly for bruiſes, and apply it outwardly to green wounds, preferring it before *Balm of Gilead*. I procur'd a Bottle of it, and have found it, upon ſome ſmall tryals, a very healing medicine. The Roſes of *Jericho* were not to be found at this ſeaſon.

Wedneſday, March 31.

This morning we all decamp'd at half an hour after two, and returning the ſame way by which we came, arriv'd in about ſix hours near the Walls of *Jeruſalem*. Our Company did not think fit to enter the City, reſolving to go immediately for *Bethlehem*. In order to which, we turn'd down into the Valley of *Jehoſaphat*; and ſo paſſing by the City, inſtantly took the Road to the place intended.

From

From *Jerusalem* to *Bethlehem*, is but two hours Travel. The Country thro' which the Road lies, is the Valley of *Rephaim*; as may be gather'd from *Jos. Ant. Lib.* 4. *Cap.* 10. A Valley so famous for being the Theatre of *David*'s Victories against the *Philistines*, 2 *Sam.* 5. 23. In the Road you meet with these following remarkable places; First, a place said to be the House of *Simeon*, that venerable old Prophet, who taking our Blessed Saviour in his Arms sung his *Nunc dimittis* in the Temple. Secondly, the famous Turpentine Tree, in the shade of which the Blessed Virgin is said to have repos'd, when she was carrying Christ in her Arms, to present him to the Lord at *Jerusalem*. Thirdly, a Convent dedicated to St. *Elias*, the impress of whose Body, the Greek Monks residing here pretend to shew in a hard Stone, which was wont to serve him for his Bed. Near this Convent also is a Well, where you are told it was that the Star appear'd to the Eastern *Magi* to their exceeding joy. Fourthly, *Rachel*'s Tomb; This may probably be the true place of her interment, mention'd *Gen.* 35. 19. But the present Sepulchral Monument can be none of that which *Jacob* erected; for it appears plainly to be a modern and Turkish Structure. Near this Monument is a little piece of ground, in which are pick'd up a little sort of small round Stones, exactly resembling Pease: concerning which they have a tradition here, that they were once truly what they now seem to be; but that the Blessed Virgin petrify'd them by a Miracle, in punishment to a surly Rustick, who deny'd her the Charity of a handful of them to relieve her hunger.

Being arriv'd at *Bethlehem*, we immediately made a circular visit to all the holy places belonging to it: as namely the place where it is said, our Blessed Lord was Born; the Manger in which it is said he was laid; the Chappel of St *Joseph* his suppos'd Father; that of the *Innocents*; those of St *Jerom*, of St *Paula* and *Eustochium*, and of *Eusebius* of *Cremona*; and lastly, the School of St *Jerom*. All which places it shall suffice just to name.

From

From the top of the Church, we had a large prospect of the adjacent Country. The most remarkable places in view were *Tekoah*, situate on the side of a Hill, about nine Miles distant to the Southward; *Engedi*, distant about three Miles Eastward; and somewhat farther off, the same way, a high sharp Hill, call'd the Mountain of the *Franks*, because defended by a Party of the Crusaders forty years after the loss of *Jerusalem.*

Thursday, April 1.

This morning we went to see some remarkable places in the neighbourhood of *Bethlehem.* The first place that we directed our course to, was those famous Fountains, Pools and Gardens, about one hour and a quarter distant from *Bethlehem* Southward, said to have been the contrivance and delight of King *Solomon.* To these works and places of pleasure that great Prince is suppos'd to allude, *Eccl.* 2. 5, 6. where amongst the other instances of his Magnificence, he reckons up his Gardens and Vineyards and Pools.

As for the Pools, they are three in number, lying in a row above each other; being so dispos'd, that the Waters of the uppermost may descend into the second, and those of the second into the third. Their figure is quadrangular; the breadth is the same in all, amounting to about ninety paces; in their length there is some difference between them; the first being about one hundred and sixty paces long, the second two hundred, the third two hundred and twenty. They are all lin'd with wall, and plaister'd, and contain a great depth of Water.

Close by the Pools is a pleasant Castle of a modern Structure; and at about the distance of one hundred and forty paces from them, is the Fountain from which principally they derive their Waters. This the Fryars will have to be that *Seal'd Fountain*, to which the holy Spouse is compar'd, *Can.* 4. 12. And, in confirmation of this opinion, they pretend a tradition, that King *Solomon* shut up these springs, and kept the door of them seal'd with

his

his Signet; to the end that he might preserve the Waters for his own drinking, in their natural freshness and purity. Nor was it difficult thus to secure them, they rising under ground, and having no avenue to them but by a little hole like to the Mouth of a narrow Well. Thro' this hole you descend directly down, but not without some difficulty, for about four yards; and then arrive in a vaulted Room, fifteen paces long, and eight broad. Joyning to this, is another Room of the same fashion, but somewhat less. Both these Rooms are cover'd with handsome stone Arches very ancient, and perhaps the work of *Solomon* himself.

You find here four places at which the Water rises: From those separate sources it is convey'd, by little rivulets, into a kind of Basin, and from thence is carried by a large subterraneous Passage down into the Pools. In the way, before it arrives at the Pools, there is an Aqueduct of brick Pipes, which receives part of the Stream, and carries it by many turnings and windings, about the Mountains, to *Jerusalem*.

Below the Pools here runs down a narrow rocky Valley, enclos'd on both sides with high Mountains. This the Fryars will have to be the enclos'd Garden, alluded to in the same place of the *Canticles* before cited. *A garden enclosed is my sister, my spouse: a spring shut up, a fountain sealed.* What truth there may be in this conjecture, I cannot absolutely pronounce. As to the Pools, it is probable enough, they may be the same with *Solomon*'s; there not being the like store of excellent Spring-Water, to be met with any where else, throughout all *Palestine*. But for the Gardens one may safely affirm, that if *Solomon* made them, in the rocky Ground which is now assigned for them, he demonstrated greater power and wealth in finishing his design, than he did wisdom in choosing the place for it.

From these memorials of *Solomon*, we returned toward *Bethlehem* again, in order to visit some places nearer home. The places we saw were, The Field where it is said the Shepherds were watching their Flocks, when they receiv'd the glad tidings of the Birth of Christ; and not far from the Field, the Village where they dwelt; and a little on the right hand of the Village, an old desolate Nunnery built by St *Paula*, and made the more memorable by her dying in it. These places are all within about half a Mile of the Convent, Eastward; and with these we finished this mornings work.

Having seen what is usually visited on the South and East of *Bethlehem*, we walk'd out after dinner to the Westward, to see what was remarkable on that side. The first place we were guided to was the Well of *David*, so call'd because held to be the same that *David* so passionately thirsted after, 2 *Sam.* 23. 15. It is a Well (or rather a Cistern) supply'd only with Rain, without any natural excellency in its Waters to make them desireable: But it seems *David*'s Spirit had a farther aim.

About two furlongs beyond this Well, are to be seen some remains of an old Aqueduct, which anciently convey'd the Waters from *Solomon*'s Pools to *Jerusalem*. This is said to be the genuine work of *Solomon*; and may well be allow'd to be in reality, what it is pretended for. It is carried all along upon the surface of the ground, and is compos'd of Stones—— foot square, and—— thick, perforated with a cavity of —— inches diameter, to make the Channel. These Stones are let into each other with a fillet fram'd round about the cavity, to prevent leakage; and united to each other with so firm a Cement, that they will sometimes sooner break (tho' a kind of course Marble) than endure a separation. This train of Stones was cover'd, for its greater security, with a case of smaller Stones, laid over it in a very strong Mortar. The whole work seems to be endued with such absolute firmness, as if it had been design'd for Eternity. But the Turks have demonstrated in this instance, that nothing can be so well wrought, but they are able to destroy it. For of this strong Aqueduct, which was carried formerly five or six leagues, with so vast expence and labour, you see now only here and there a fragment remaining. Re-

Returning from this place we went to see the Greek and Armenian Convents; which are contiguous to that of the Latins, and have each their several doors opening into the Chappel of the holy Manger. The next place we went to see was the Grot of the Blessed Virgin. It is within thirty or forty yards of the Convent; and is reverenced upon the account of a tradition that the Blessed Virgin here hid her self and her Divine Babe from the fury of *Herod*, for some time before their departure into *Egypt*. The Grot is hollow'd into a Chalky Rock: But this whiteness they will have to be not natural, but to have been occasion'd by some miraculous drops of the Blessed Virgin's Milk, which fell from her Breast while she was suckling the holy Infant. And so much are they possess'd with this opinion, that they believe the chalk of this Grotto has a miraculous virtue for encreasing Women's milk. And I was assured from many hands, that it is very frequently taken by the Women hereabouts, as well Turks and Arabs, as Christians, for that purpose, and that with very good effect; which perhaps may be true enough, it being well known how much Fancy is wont to do in things of this nature.

Friday, April 2.

The next morning presenting the Guardian with two Chequeens a piece for his civilities to us, we took our leaves of *Bethlehem*, designing just to go visit the Wilderness and Convent of St *John Baptist*, and so return to *Jerusalem*.

In this Stage we first cross'd part of that famous Valley, in which it is said that the Angel in one night did such prodigious execution, in the Army of *Sennacherib*. Having travell'd about half an hour, we came to a Village call'd *Booteshellah*; concerning which they relate this remarkable property, that no Turk can live in it above two years. By virtue of this report, whether true or false, the Christians keep the Village to themselves without molestation; no Turk being willing to stake his life in experimenting the truth of it. In somewhat less than an hour more we came to the Fountain, where they told us, but falsly, that *Philip* baptized the Æthiopian *Eunuch*. The Passage here is so rocky and uneven, that pilgrims finding how difficult the road is for a single Horseman, are ready to think it impossible that a Chariot (such as the *Eunuch* rode in, *Acts* 8. 28.) should ever have been able to go this way. But it must not be judged what the Road was in ancient times, by what the negligence of the Turks has now reduced it to: for I observ'd not far from the Fountain, a place where the Rock had been cut away in old time, in order to lay open a good Road; by which it may be suppos'd that the same care was used all along this Passage, tho' now time and negligence have obliterated both the fruit and almost the signs of such labour.

A little beyond this Fountain, we came to that which they call the Village of St *Philip*; at which ascending a very steep Hill, we arrived at the Wilderness of St *John*: A Wilderness it is call'd, as being very Rocky and Mountainous; but is well cultivated, and produces plenty of Corn and Vines and Olive Trees. After a good hours travel in this Wilderness, we came to the Cave and Fountain, where, as they say, the *Baptist* exercis'd those severe austerities related of him, *Matt.* 3. 4. Near this Cell there still grow some old Locust Trees, the Monuments of the Ignorance of the middle times. These the Fryars aver to be the very same that yielded sustenance to the *Baptist*, and the Popish Pilgrims, who dare not be wiser than such blind guides, gather the fruit of them, and carry it away with great devotion.

Having done with this place, we directed our course toward the Convent of St *John*, which is about a league distant Eastward. In our way we pass'd along one side of the Valley of *Elah*, where *David* slew the Giant, that Defyer of the Army of *Israel*, 1 *Sam.* 17. We had likewise in sight *Modon*, a Village on the top of a high Hill, the burying place of those Heroical Defenders of their Country, the *Maccabees*.

Being

Being come near the Convent, we were led a little out of the way, to visit a place, which they call the House of *Elizabeth* the Mother of the *Baptist*. This was formerly a Convent also: but it is now a heap of ruins, and the only remarkable place left in it is a Grotto, in which (you are told) it was, that the Blessed Virgin saluted *Elizabeth*, and pronounc'd her divine *Magnificat*, *Luke* 1. 46.

The present Convent of St *John*, which is now inhabited, stands at about three furlongs distance from this House of *Elizabeth*; and is suppos'd to be built at the place where St *John* was Born. If you chance to ask, how it came to pass, that *Elizabeth* liv'd in one House, when she was big with the *Baptist*, and in another when she brought him forth? The answer you are like to receive, is, that the former was her Country, the latter her City Habitation; and that it is no wonder for a Wife of one of the Priests of better rank (such as she was, *Luke* 1. 6.) to be provided with such variety.

The Convent of St *John* has been, within these four years, rebuilt from the ground. It is at present a large square Building, uniform and neat all over; but that which is most eminently beautiful in it, is its Church. It consists of three Isles, and has in the middle a handsom Cupola, under which is a pavement of Mosaick, equal to, if not exceeding the finest works of the Ancients in that kind. At the upper end of the North Isle, you go down seven Marble Steps, to a very splendid Altar, erected over the very place where they say the holy *Baptist* was born. Here are Artificers still employ'd, in adding farther beauty and ornament to this Convent; and yet it has been so expensive a work already, that the Fryars themselves give out, there is not a Stone laid in it but has cost them a Dollar: which, considering the large Sums exacted by the Turks for Licence to begin Fabricks of this nature, and also their perpetual Extortion and Avarrias afterwards, besides the necessary charge of Building, may be allow'd to pass for no extravagant Hyperbole.

Returning

Returning from St *John*'s toward *Jerusalem*, we came in about three quarters of an hour to a Convent of the Greeks, taking its Name from the holy Crofs. This Convent is very neat in its ftructure, and in its fituation delightful. But that which moft deferves to be noted in it, is the reafon of its Name and Foundation. It is becaufe here is the Earth, that nourifhed the Root, that bore the Tree, that yielded the Timber that made the Crofs. Under the high Altar you are fhewn a hole in the ground where the ftump of the Tree ftood, and it meets with not a few Vifitants fo much veryer ftocks than it felf, as to fall down and worfhip it. This Convent is not above half an hour from *Jerufalem*; to which place we return'd this evening, being the fifth day fince our departure thence.

After our return, we were invited into the Convent, to have our feet wafh'd; A Ceremony perform'd to each Pilgrim by the Father Guardian himfelf. The whole Society ftands round, finging fome Latin Hymns, all the while the Father Guardian is doing his office: And when he has done every Fryar comes in order, and kiffes the feet of the Pilgrim. All this was perform'd with great order and folemnity: And if it ferved either to teftify a fincere humility and charity in them, or to improve thofe excellent Graces in others, it might pafs for no unufeful Ceremony.

Saturday, *April* 3.

We went about midday to fee the function of the *Holy Fire*. This is a Ceremony kept up by the Greeks and Armenians, upon a perfwafion, that every Eafter Eve there is a Miraculous Flame defcends from Heaven into the holy Sepulcher, and kindles all the Lamps and Candles there, as the Sacrifice was burnt at the Prayers of *Elijah*, 1 *Kings* 18.

Coming to the Church of the holy Sepulcher, we found it crowded with a numerous and diftracted Mob, making a hideous clamour very unfit for that facred place, and better becoming Bacchanals than Chriftians. Getting with

fome

ſome ſtruggle thro' this crowd, we went up into the Gallery on that ſide of the Church next the Latin Convent, whence we could diſcern all that paſs'd in this religious frenzy.

They began their diſorders by running round the holy Sepulcher with all their might and ſwiftneſs, crying out as they went, *Huia*, which ſignifies *this is he*, or *this is it*; an expreſſion by which they aſſert the verity of the Chriſtian Religion. After they had by theſe vertiginous circulations and clamours turn'd their heads, and inflam'd their madneſs, they began to act the moſt antick tricks and poſtures, in a thouſand ſhapes of diſtraction. Sometimes they dragg'd one another along the floor all round the Sepulcher; ſometimes they ſet one Man upright on another's ſhoulders, and in this poſture march'd round; ſometimes they took Men with their heels upward, and hurry'd them about in ſuch an undecent manner, as to expoſe their Nudities; ſometimes they tumbled round the Sepulcher, after the manner of Tumblers on the Stage. In a word, nothing can be imagin'd more rude or extravagant, than what was acted upon this occaſion.

In this tumultuous frantick humour they continued from twelve 'till four of the Clock: the reaſon of which delay was, becauſe of a Suit that was then in debate before the Cadi, betwixt the Greeks and Armenians; the former endeavouring to exclude the latter from having any ſhare in this Miracle. Both Parties having expended (as I was inform'd) five thouſand Dollars between them, in this fooliſh Controverſy; the Cadi at laſt gave ſentence, that they ſhould enter the holy Sepulcher together, as had been uſual at former times. Sentence being thus given, at four of the Clock both Nations went on with their Ceremony. The Greeks firſt ſet out, in a proceſſion round the holy Sepulcher, and immediately at their heels follow'd the Armenians. In this order they compaſs'd the holy Sepulcher thrice, having produc'd all their Gallantry of Standards, Streamers, Crucifixes and Embroider'd Habits upon this occaſion.

Toward

Toward the end of this proceſſion, there was a Pigeon came fluttering into the Cupola over the Sepulcher; at ſight of which, there was a greater ſhout and clamour than before. This Bird, the Latins told us, was purpoſely let fly by the Greeks, to deceive the people into an opinion that it was a viſible deſcent of the Holy Ghoſt.

The proceſſion being over, the Suffragan of the Greek Patriarch (he being himſelf at *Conſtantinople*,) and the Principal Armenian Biſhop approach'd to the door of the Sepulcher, and cutting the ſtring with which it was faſtned and ſeal'd, enter'd in, ſhutting the door after them; all the Candles and Lamps within having been before extinguiſh'd, in the preſence of the Turks and other witneſſes. The exclamations were doubled, as the Miracle drew nearer to its accompliſhment; and the People preſs'd with ſuch vehemence towards the door of the Sepulcher, that it was not in the power of the Turks, ſet to guard it, with the ſevereſt drubs, to keep them off. The cauſe of their preſſing in this manner, is the great deſire they have to light their Candles at the holy Flame, as ſoon as it is firſt brought out of the Sepulcher; it being eſteem'd the moſt ſacred and pure, as coming immediately from Heaven.

The two Miracle-Mongers had not been above a minute in the holy Sepulcher, when the glimmering of the holy Fire was ſeen, or imagin'd to appear, thro' ſome chinks of the door; and certainly Bedlam it ſelf never ſaw ſuch an unruly tranſport, as was produc'd in the Mob at this ſight.

Immediately after, out came the two Prieſts with blazing Torches in their hands, which they held up at the door of the Sepulcher, while the People throng'd about with inexpreſſible ardour; every one ſtriving to obtain a part of the firſt and pureſt Flame. The Turks in the mean time, with huge Clubs, laid them on without mercy; but all this could not repel them, the exceſs of their tranſport making them inſenſible of pain. Thoſe that got the Fire applied it immediately to their Beards, Faces and Boſoms,

pretending

pretending that it would not burn like an Earthly Flame: but I plainly saw, none of them could endure this experiment long enough to make good that pretension.

So many hands being employ'd, you may be sure, it could not be long before innumerable Tapers were lighted. The whole Church, Gallerys, and every place seemed instantly to be in a Flame; and with this Illumination the Ceremony ended.

It must be own'd, that those two within the Sepulcher, perform'd their part with great quickness and dexterity: but the behaviour of the Rabble without, very much discredited the Miracle. The Latins take a great deal of pains to expose this Ceremony, as a most shameful imposture, and a scandal to the Christian Religion; perhaps out of envy, that others should be Masters of so gainful a business; but the Greeks and Armenians pin their Faith upon it, and make their Pilgrimages chiefly upon this motive: and 'tis the deplorable unhappiness of their Priests, that having acted the cheat so long already, they are forc'd now to stand to it, for fear of endangering the Apostacy of their People.

Going out of the Church, after the rout was over, we saw several People gather'd about the Stone of Unction, who having got a good store of Candles, lighted with the holy Fire, were employ'd in dawbing pieces of Linnen with the Wicks of them and the melting Wax; which pieces of Linnen were design'd for Winding-sheets: and 'tis the opinion of these poor People, that if they can but have the happiness to be buried in a shroud smutted with this Celestial Fire, it will certainly secure them from the Flames of Hell.

Sunday, April 4.

This day being our Easter, we did not go abroad to visit any places, the time requiring an employment of another nature.

Monday, April 5.

This morning we went to see some more of the Curiosities which had been yet unvisited by us. The first place we came to was that which they call St *Peter's* Prison, from which he was deliver'd by the Angel, *Acts* 12. It is close by the Church of the holy Sepulcher, and still serves for its Primitive use. About the space of a furlong from thence, we came to an old Church, held to have been built by *Helena*, in the place where stood the House of *Zebedee*. This is in the hands of the Greeks, who tell you, that *Zebedee* being a Fisherman was wont to bring Fish from *Joppa* hither, and to vend it at this place. Not far from hence we came to the place where, they say, stood anciently the Iron Gate, which open'd to *Peter* of its own accord. A few steps farther, is the small Church built over the House of *Mark*, to which the Apostle directed his course, after his miraculous Goal-delivery. The Syrians (who have this place in their custody) pretend to shew you the very Window at which *Rhoda* look'd out, while *Peter* knock'd at the door. In the Church they shew a Syriack Manuscript of the New Testament in Folio, pretended to be eight hundred and fifty two years old; and a little Stone Font used by the Apostles themselves in Baptizing. About one hundred and fifty paces farther in the same Street, is that which they call the House of St *Thomas*, converted formerly into a Church, but now a Mosque. Not many paces farther, is another Street crossing the former, which leads you on the right hand to the place, where they say our Lord appear'd, after his Resurrection, to the three *Marys*, *Matth*. 28. 9. Three *Marys* the Fryars tell you, tho' in that place of St *Matthew* mention is made but of two. The same Street carries you on the left hand to the Armenian Convent. The Armenians have here a very large and delightful space of ground; their Convent and Gardens taking up all that part of *Mount Sion*, which is within the Walls of the City. Their Church is built over the place where, they say, St *James* the Brother of *John*

was

was Beheaded, *Acts* 12. 2. In a ſmall Chappel on the North ſide of the Church, is ſhewn the very place of his Decollation. In this Church are two Altars ſet out with extraordinary ſplendour, being deck'd with rich Mitres, Embroider'd Copes, Croſſes both Silver and Gold, Crowns, Chalices, and other Church Utenſils without number. In the middle of the Church is a Pulpit made of Tortoiſe-ſhell, and Mother of Pearl, with a beautiful Canopy, or Cupola over it, of the ſame Fabrick. The Tortoiſe-ſhell and Mother of Pearl are ſo exquiſitely mingled and inlaid in each other, that the work far exceeds the materials. In a kind of Anti-Chappel to this Church, there are laid up on one ſide of an Altar, three large rough Stones, eſteem'd very precious; as being, one of them, the Stone upon which *Moſes* caſt the two Tables, when he broke them, in Indignation, at the Idolatry of the *Iſraelites*; the other two being brought, one from the place of our Lord's Baptiſm, the other from that of his Transfiguration.

Leaving this Convent, we went a little farther to another ſmall Church, which was likewiſe in the hands of the Armenians. This is ſuppos'd to be founded in the place where *Annas*'s Houſe ſtood. Within the Church, not far from the door, is ſhewn a hole in the Wall, denoting the place where one of the Officers of the high Prieſt ſmote our Bleſſed Saviour, *John* 18. 22. The Officer, by whoſe impious hand that Buffet was given, the Fryars will have to be the ſame *Malchus*, whoſe Ear our Lord had heal'd. In the Court before this Chappel is an Olive Tree, of which it is reported, that Chriſt was chain'd to it for ſome time by order of *Annas* to ſecure him from eſcaping.

From the Houſe of *Annas* we were conducted out of *Sion* Gate, which is near adjoyning to that which they call the Houſe of *Cajaphas*, where is another ſmall Chappel belonging alſo to the Armenians. Here, under the Altar, they tell us is depoſited that very Stone, which was laid to ſecure the door of our Saviour's Sepulcher, *Mat.* 27. 60. It was a long time kept in the Church of the Sepulcher;

but the Armenians, not many years ſince, ſtole it from thence by a ſtratagem, and convey'd it to this place. The Stone is two yards and a quarter long, high one yard, and broad as much. It is plaiſter'd all over, except in five or ſix little places, where it is left bare to receive the immediate kiſſes and other devotions of Pilgrims. Here is likewiſe ſhewn a little Cell ſaid to have been our Lord's Priſon, 'till the morning when he was carried from hence before *Pilate*; and alſo the place where *Peter* was frighted into a denial of his Maſter.

A little farther without the Gate is the Church of the *Cœnaculum*, where they ſay Chriſt inſtituted his laſt Supper. It is now a Moſque, and not to be ſeen by Chriſtians. Near this is a Well, which is ſaid to marke out the place at which the Apoſtles divided from each other, in order to go every Man to his ſeveral Charge; and cloſe by the Well are the ruins of a Houſe in which the Bleſſed Virgin is ſuppos'd to have breath'd her laſt. Going Eaſtward a little way down the Hill, we were ſhewn the place where a Jew arreſted the Corps of the Bleſſed Virgin, as ſhe was carry'd to her Interment; for which impious preſumption, he had his hand wither'd wherewith he had ſeiz'd the Bier. About as much lower in the middle of the Hill, they ſhew you the Grot, in which St *Peter* wept ſo bitterly for his inconſtancy to his Lord.

We extended our Circuit no farther at this time; but enter'd the City again at *Sion* Gate. Turning down as ſoon as we had enter'd, on the right hand, and going about two furlongs cloſe by the City Wall, we were had into a Garden, lying at the foot of *Mount Moriah*, on the South ſide. Here we were ſhewn ſeveral large Vaults, annext to the Mountain on this ſide, and running at leaſt fifty yards under ground. They were built in two Iſles, arch'd at top with huge firm Stone, and ſuſtain'd with tall Pillars conſiſting each of one ſingle Stone, and two yards in diameter. This might poſſibly be ſome under-ground work made to enlarge the Area of the Temple: For *Joſephus* ſeems to deſcribe ſome ſuch work as this, erected over the

Valley on this side of the Temple, *Ant. Jud. Lib.* 15. *Cap. ult.*

From these Vaults, we return'd toward the Convent. In our way, we pass'd thro' the Turkish *Bazars*, and took a view of the *Beautiful Gate* of the Temple. But we could but just view it in passing, it not being safe to stay here long, by reason of the superstition of the Turks.

Tuesday, Apr. 6.

The next morning we took another progress about the City. We made our Exit at *Bethlehem* Gate, and turning down on the left hand under the Castle of the *Pisans*, came in about a furlong and a half to that which they call *Bathsheba*'s Pool. It lies at the bottom of *Mount Sion*, and is suppos'd to be the same in which *Bathsheba* was washing her self, when *David* spied her from the Terrace of his Pallace. But others refer this accident to another lesser Pool in a Garden, just within *Bethlehem* Gate; and perhaps both opinions are equally in the right.

A little below this Pool, begins the Valley of *Hinnom*; on the West side of which is the place call'd anciently the *Potters Field*, and afterwards the *Field of Blood*, from its being purchas'd with the pieces of Silver which were the Price of the Blood of Christ: But at present, from that veneration which it has obtain'd amongst Christians, it is call'd *Campo Sancto*. It is a small plat of ground, not above thirty yards long, and about half as much broad. One moiety of it is taken up by a square Fabrick twelve yards high, built for a Charnel House. The Corpses are let down into it from the top, there being five holes left open for that purpose. Looking down thro' these holes we could see many Bodies under several degrees of decay; from which it may be conjectur'd, that this Grave does not make that quick dispatch with the Corpses committed to it, which is commonly reported. The Armenians have the command of this Burying place, for which they pay the Turks a Rent of one Zequin a day. The Earth is of a chalky substance hereabouts.

A little

A little below the *Campo Sancto*, is shewn an intricate Cave or Sepulcher, consisting of several Rooms one within another, in which the *Apostles* are said to have hid themselves, when they forsook their Master, and fled. The entrance of the Cave discovers signs of its having been adorn'd with Painting in ancient times.

A little farther the Valley of *Hinnom* terminates, that of *Jehosaphat* running cross the Mouth of it. Along the bottom of this latter Valley runs the Brook *Cedron*; a Brook in Winter-time, but without the least drop of water in it all the time we were at *Jerusalem*.

In the Valley of *Jehosaphat*, the first thing you are carried to is the Well of *Nehemiah*; so call'd because reputed to be the same place from which that Restorer of *Israel* recover'd the Fire of the Altar, after the Babylonish Captivity, 2 *Macc*.1.19. A little higher in the Valley, on the left hand, you come to a Tree, suppos'd to mark out the place where the *Evangelical Prophet* was sawn asunder. About one hundred paces higher, on the same side, is the Pool of *Siloam*. It was anciently dignified with a Church built over it: but when we were there, a Tanner made no scruple to dress his hides in it. Going about a furlong farther on the same side, you come to the Fountain of the *Blessed Virgin*, so call'd, because she was wont (as is reported) to resort hither for water; but at what time, and upon what occasions, it is not yet agreed. Over against this Fountain on the other side of the Valley, is a Village call'd *Siloe*, in which *Solomon* is said to have kept his strange Wives; and above the Village is a Hill call'd the *Mountain of Offence*, because there *Solomon* built the high places mention'd, 1 *Kings* 11. 7. his Wives having perverted his wise heart, to follow their Idolatrous Abominations in his declining years. On the same side, and not far distant from *Siloe*, they shew another *Aceldama* or *Field of Blood*; so call'd, because there it was that *Judas*, by the just judgment of God, met with his compounded death, *Mat*. 27. 5. *Acts* 1. 18, 19. A little farther on the same side of the Valley, they shew'd us several Jewish Monu-

Beſchryvinghe van de Kercke, daer de heylighe Moeder Godts ; S. Joſeph haren Bruydegom, de HH. Joachim, ende Anna haer eerweerdige Ouders begraven zyn gheweeſt.

Verklaringhe van de plate des Grafs van onſe lieve Vrouwe.

1. Den Ingang van de Kercke ende de Trappen.
2. De Ciſterne in 't portael van de Kercke.
3. Het Graf van onſe lieve Vrouwe.
4. Autaer der Griecken.
5. Moſquit daer de Turken hun ghebedt doen.
6. De Begraeffeniſſe van ſint Joſeph.
7. De Graven van S. Joachim, ende S. Anna.
8. Den Autaer der Armenẽ.
9. De Deure van de Kercke.
10. Eẽ Venſter ſtaende naer den Ooſten van de kerke.
11. Ingang der Speloncke, komende in den Hof van Oliveten.
12. Het fatſoen van de Speloncke.
13. Het Voor-portael van de kercke.
14. Den Hof van een Turck in 't Hofken van Olivetẽ.
15. Openinge in de Speloncke, waer door ſy haer licht ſchept.
16. Den Olyf-bergh.

HET GRAF VAN ONSE L.VROUWE. Pag. 514.

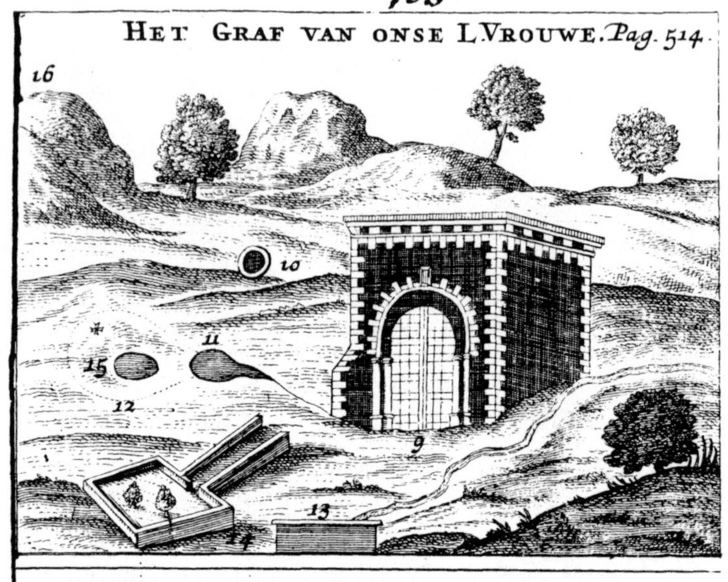

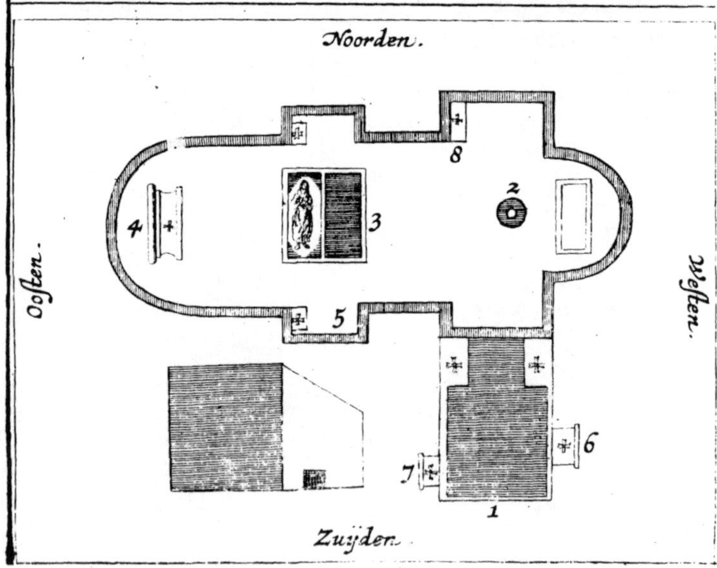

Monuments. Amongst the rest there are two noble Antiquities, which they call the Sepulcher of *Zachary*, and the Pillar of *Absolom*. Close by the latter, is the Sepulcher of *Jehosaphat*, from which the whole Valley takes its Name.

Upon the edge of the Hill, on the opposite side of the Valley, there runs along in a direct line, the Wall of the City. Near the corner of which, there is a short end of a Pillar, jetting out of the Wall. Upon this Pillar the Turks have a tradition that *Mahomet* shall sit in Judgment, at the last day; and that all the World shall be gathered together in the Valley below, to receive their doom from his Mouth. A little farther Northward is the Gate of the Temple. It is at present wall'd up, because the Turks here have a Prophecy, that their destruction shall enter at that Gate; the completion of which prediction they endeavour by this means to prevent. Below this Gate, in the bottom of the Valley, is a broad hard Stone, discovering several impressions upon it, which you may fancy to be Footsteps. These the Fryars tell you are Prints made by our Blessed Saviour's Feet, when, after his Apprehension, he was hurried violently away to the Tribunal of his Blood-thirsty Persecutors.

From hence, keeping still in the bottom of the Valley, you come in a few paces to a place, which they call the Sepulcher of the *Blessed Virgin*. It has a magnificent descent down into it of forty seven Stairs: On the right hand, as you go down, is the Sepulcher of St *Anna* the Mother, and on the left, that of St *Joseph* the Husband of the Blessed Virgin.

Having finish'd our visit to this place, we went up the Hill toward the City. In the side of the ascent, we were shewn a broad Stone on which they say St *Stephen* suffer'd Martyrdom; and not far from it is a Grot, into which they tell you the outragious Jewish Zealots cast his Body, when they had satiated their fury upon him. From hence we went immediately to St *Stephen*'s Gate, so call'd from its Vicinity to this place of the Protomartyr's suffering; and so return'd to our Lodging.

Wednesday,

Wednesday, April 7.

The next morning we ſet out again, in order to ſee the Sanctuaries, and other viſitable places upon *Mount Olivet.* We went out at St *Stephen*'s Gate, and croſſing the Valley of *Jehoſaphat*, began immediately to aſcend the Mountains. Being got about two thirds of the way up, we came to certain Grottos cut with intricate Windings and Caverns under ground: Theſe are call'd the Sepulchers of the *Prophets.* A little higher up, are twelve arch'd Vaults under ground, ſtanding ſide by ſide; theſe were built in memory of the twelve *Apoſtles*, who are ſaid to have compil'd their Creed in this place. Sixty paces higher you come to the place, where they ſay Chriſt utter'd his Prophecy concerning the final deſtruction of *Jeruſalem, Mat.* 2. 4. And a little on the right hand of this, is the place where they ſay he dictated a ſecond time the *Pater noſter* to his diſciples, *Luke* 11. 1, 2. Somewhat higher is the Cave of St *Pelagia*; and as much more above that, a Pillar, ſignifying the place where an Angel gave the Bleſſed Virgin three days warning of her Death. At the top of the Hill, you come to the place of our Bleſſed Lord's Aſcenſion. Here was anciently a large Church, built in honour of that glorious Triumph: But all that now remains of it is only an octogonal Cupola, about eight yards in diameter, ſtanding, as they ſay, over the very place, where were ſet the laſt Footſteps of the Son of God here on Earth. Within the Cupola there is ſeen, in a hard ſtone, as they tell you, the print of one of his Feet. Here was alſo that of the other Foot ſometime ſince; but it has been remov'd from hence by the Turks into the great Moſque upon *Mount Moriah.* This Chappel of the Aſcenſion, the Turks have the cuſtody of, and uſe it for a Moſque. There are many other holy places about *Jeruſalem*, which the Turks pretend to have a veneration for, equally with the Chriſtians; and under that pretence they take them into their own hands. But whether they do this out of real devotion, or for lucre's ſake, and to the end that they may

exact

Pag. 5

DE CAPELLE VAN ONS HEEREN HEMEL-VAERT.

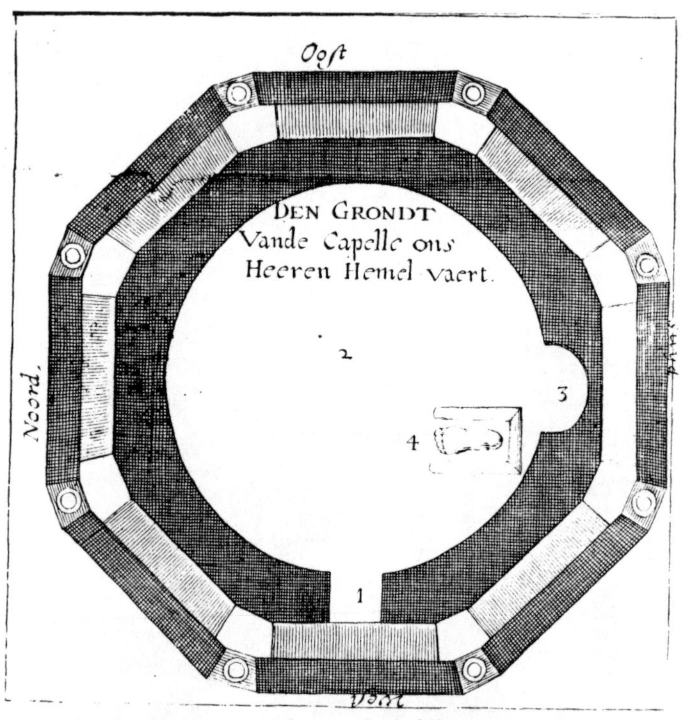

Bedietſel van het cyfer in de Grond-plate.

1. De poorte van de Capel.
2. De Capelle.
3. Het rondeel dienende de Turcken voor Moſquit.
4. Den Voet-ſtap onſes Saligh-makers.

Vytlegginghe van den Olyf-bergh.

A. Daer Christus ten Hemel voer.

B. Den kelder van Pelagia.

C. Daer Christus sprack van den dagh des Oordeels.

D. Daer hy het Vader ons leerde.

E. Daer d' Apostelen het Geloof stelden.

F. Daer Christus over de stadt weende.

G. Daer de H. Maget ruste.

O. Gethsemani.

P. Het graf van de H. Maghet Maria.

Q. Daer Judas sich verhing

R. Den pilaer Absalons.

S. De brugh die over Cedron light.

T. Graven der Joden.

H. Daer den Engel sprack: *Ghy Mannen van Galileen, &c.*

I. Daer S. Tomas des Heyl. Magets gordel op-nam.

K. Daer de H. Maghet sat, aenschouwende de martelisatie vã S Stephanus.

L. Daer Christus syn dry Discipelen liet.

M. Daer hy gevangen wirt.

N. De Cap van Christi be- [illegible]

V. Het dal des vervloeckten vyghe booms.

X. Den wegh naer Betania.

Y. Den wegh naer Jerusalem.

Z De beke Cedron.

✠ Den bergh der vertoornissen.

exact Money from the Christians for admission into them, I will not determine.

About two furlongs from this place Northward, is the highest part of *Mount Olivet*; and upon that was anciently erected an high Tower, in memory of that Apparition of the two Angels to the Apostles, after our Blessed Lord's Ascension, *Acts* 1. 10, 11. from which the Tower it self had the Name given it of *Viri Galilæi*! This ancient Monument remain'd 'till about two years since, when it was demolish'd by a Turk, who had bought the Field in which it stood: But neverthelesss you have still, from the natural height of the place, a large prospect of *Jerusalem*, and the adjacent Country, and of the *Dead Sea*, &c.

From this place, we descended the Mount again by another road. At about the midway down, they shew you the place where Christ beheld the City, and wept over it, *Luke* 19.41. Near the bottom of the Hill is a great Stone, upon which, you are told, the Blessed Virgin let fall her Girdle after her Assumption, in order to convince St. *Thomas*, who, they say, was troubled with a fit of his old Incredulity upon this occasion. There is still to be seen a small winding channel upon the Stone, which they will have to be the impression made by the Girdle when it fell, and to be left for the conviction of all such as shall suspect the truth of their Story of the Assumption.

About twenty yards lower they shew you *Gethsemane*; an even plat of ground, not above fifty seven yards square, lying between the foot of *Mount Olivet* and the brook *Cedron*. It is well planted with Olive Trees, and those of so old a growth, that they are believ'd to be the same that stood here in our Blessed Saviour's time. In vertue of which persuasion, the Olives, and Olive stones, and Oyl which they produce, became an excellent commodity in *Spain*. But that these Trees cannot be so ancient as is pretended, is evident from what *Josephus* testifies, *Lib.* 7. *Bell. Jud. Cap.* 15. and in other places, *viz.* that *Titus* in his Siege of *Jerusalem*, cut down all the Trees within about one hundred furlongs of *Jerusalem*; and that the

Souldiers were forced to fetch Wood so far, for making their Mounts, when they Assaulted the Temple.

At the upper corner of the Garden is a flat naked ledge of Rock, reputed to be the place, on which the Apostles, *Peter*, *James* and *John*, fell a sleep during the Agony of our Lord. And a few paces from hence is a Grotto, said to be the place, in which Christ underwent that bitter part of his Passion.

About eight paces from the place where the Apostles slept, is a small shred of ground twelve yards long, and one broad, suppos'd to be the very Path on which the Traitor *Judas* walk'd up to Christ, saying, *Hail Master, and kissed him*. This narrow Path is separated by a Wall out of the midst of the Garden, as a *Terra damnata*; a work the more remarkable, as being done by the Turks, who, as well as Christians, detest the very ground on which was acted such an infamous Treachery.

From hence we cross'd the Brook *Cedron*, close by the reputed Sepulcher of the Blessed Virgin; and entring at St *Stephen*'s Gate, return'd again to the Convent.

Thursday, April 8.

We went to see the Palace of *Pilate*, I mean the place where they say it stood, for now an ordinary Turkish House possesses its room. It is not far from the Gate of St *Stephen*, and borders upon the Area of the Temple on the North side. From the Terrace of this House you have a fair prospect of all the place where the Temple stood; indeed the only good prospect, that is allow'd you of it: for there is no going within the borders of it, without forfeiting your Life, or, which is worse, your Religion. A fitter place for an August Building could not be found in the whole World than this Area. It lies upon the top of *Mount Moriah* over against *Mount Olivet*, the Valley of *Jehosaphat* lying between both Mountains. It is, as far as I could compute by walking round it without, five hundred and seventy of my paces in length, and three hundred and seventy in breadth; and one may still discern marks

marks of the great labour that it cost, to cut away the hard Rock, and to level such a spacious Area upon so strong a Mountain. In the middle of the Area stands at present a Mosque of an octogonal figure, suppos'd to be built upon the same ground, where anciently stood the *Sanctum Sanctorum*. It is neither eminent for its largeness, nor its Structure; and yet it makes a very stately figure, by the sole advantage of its situation.

In this pretended House of Pilate is shewn the Room in which Christ was mock'd with the Ensigns of Royalty, and buffeted by the Soldiers. At the coming out of the House is a descent, where was anciently the *Scala Sancta*. On the other side of the Street (which was anciently part of the Palace also) is the Room where they say our Lord was scourg'd. It was once us'd for a Stable by the Son of a certain *Bassa* of *Jerusalem*: But presently upon this profanation, they say, there came such a mortality amongst his Horses, as forc'd him to resign the place. By which means it was redeem'd from that sordid use: but nevertheless, when we were there, it was no better than a Weaver's Shop. In our return from *Pilate*'s Palace, we pass'd along the *Dolourous way*; in which walk, we were shewn in order: First, the place where *Pilate* brought our Lord forth, to present to the People, with this mystick Saying, *Behold the Man*! Secondly, where Christ fainted thrice, under the weight of his Cross: Thirdly, where the Blessed Virgin swoon'd away at so tragical a Spectacle: Fourthly, where St *Veronica* presented to him the Handkerchief to wipe his bleeding Brows: Fifthly, where the Soldiers compell'd *Simon* the *Cyrenian* to bear his Cross. All which places I need only to name.

Friday, April 9.

We went to take a view of that which they call the Pool of *Bethesda*. It is one hundred and twenty paces long, and forty broad, and at least eight deep, but void of Water. At its West end it discovers some old Arches, now damm'd up. These some will have to be the five

Porches in which sate that Multitude of lame, halt and blind, *Joh.* 5. but the mischief is, instead of five, there are but three of them. This Pool is contiguous on one side, to St *Stephen*'s Gate, on the other, to the Area of the Temple.

From hence we went to the Convent or Nunnery of St *Anne*. The Church here is large and entire, and so are part of the Lodgings; but both are desolate and neglected. In a Grotto under the Church is shewn the place, where, they say, the Blessed Virgin was born. Near this Church they shew the *Pharisee*'s House, where *Mary Magdalen* exhibited those admirable evidences of a penitent affection towards our Saviour; *washing his feet with her tears, and wiping them with her hair, Luke* 7. 38. This place also has been anciently dignified with holy Buildings, but they are now neglected.

This was our morning's work. In the afternoon we went to see *Mount Gihon*, and the Pool of the same Name. It lies about two furlongs without *Bethlehem* Gate Westward. It is a stately Pool, one hundred and six paces long, and sixty seven broad, and lin'd with wall and plaister; and was, when we were there, well stor'd with water.

Saturday, April 10.

We went to take our leaves of the holy Sepulcher, this being the last time that it was to be open'd this Festival.

Upon this finishing day, and the night following, the Turks allow free admittance for all People, without demanding any fee for entrance as at other times; calling it a day of Charity. By this promiscuous Licence, they let in not only the poor, but, as I was told, the lewd and vicious also; who come hither to get convenient opportunity for prostitution, prophaning the holy places in such a manner (as it is said) that they were not worse defil'd even then when the Heathens here celebrated their *Aphrodisia*.

Sunday, April 11.

Now began the Turks *Byram*, that is, the Feast which they celebrate after their Lent, call'd by them *Ramadam*.

This

This being a time of great Libertinism among the Rabble, we thought it prudent to confine our selves to our Lodgings for some time, to the end that we might avoid such Insolencies as are usual in such times of publick Festivity. Our confinement was the less incommodious, because there was hardly any thing, either within or about the City, which we had not already visited.

Monday, April 12. *Tuesday, April* 13.

We kept close to our Quarters, but however not in idleness; the time being now come, when we were to contrive, and provide things in order for our departure. We had a bad account, from all hands, of the Country's being more and more embroyl'd by the Arabs: Which made us somewhat unresolv'd what way and method to take for our return. But during our suspence it was told us, that the Mosolem was likewise upon his return to his Master, the *Bassa* of *Tripoli*: Upon which intelligence we resolv'd, if possible, to joyn our selves to his Company.

Wednesday, April 14.

We went with a small Present in our hands to wait upon the Mosolem, in order to enquire the time of his departure, and acquaint him with our desire to go under his protection. He assur'd us of his setting out the next morning; so we immediately took our leaves in order to prepare our selves for accompanying him.

I was willing before our departure to measure the Circuit of the City: So taking one of the Fryars with me, I went out in the afternoon, in order to pace the Walls round. We went out at *Bethlehem* Gate, and proceeding on the right hand came about to the same Gate again. I found the whole City 4630 paces in Circumference; which I computed thus.

Paces

	Paces
From *Bethlehem* Gate to the corner on the right hand	400
From that corner to *Damascus* Gate	680
From *Damascus* Gate to *Herod's*	380
From *Herod's* Gate to *Jeremiah's* Prison	150
From *Jeremiah's* Prison to the corner next the Valley of *Jehosaphat*	225
From that corner to St *Stephen's* Gate	385
From St *Stephen's* Gate to the *Golden* Gate	240
From the *Golden* Gate to the corner of the Wall	380
From that corner to the *Dung* Gate	470
From the *Dung* Gate to *Sion Gate*	605
From *Sion* Gate to the corner of the Wall	215
From that corner to *Bethlehem* Gate	500
In all, Paces	4630

The reduction of my paces to yards, is by casting away a tenth part, ten of my paces making nine yards; by which reckoning the 4630 paces amount to 4167 yards, which make just two miles and a half.

Thursday, April 15.

This morning our Diplomata were presented us by the Father Guardian, to certify our having visited all the holy places; and we presented the Convent fifty Dollars a Man, as a gratuity for their trouble: Which offices having past betwixt us, we took our leaves.

We set out together with the Mosolem, and proceeding in the same Road, by which we came, lodged the first night at *Kane Leban.* But the Mosolem left us here, and continued his Stage as far as *Naplosa*; so we saw him no more. The Country People were now every where at plough in the Fields, in order to sow Cotton. 'Twas observable that in ploughing they us'd Goads of an extraordinary size. Upon measuring of several, I found them about eight foot long, and at the bigger End six inches in circumference. They were arm'd at the lesser End with a sharp Prickle for driving the Oxen, and at the other end with

with a ſmall Spade, or Paddle of Iron, ſtrong and maſſy, for cleanſing the Plough from the clay that encumbers it in working. May we not from hence conjecture, that it was with ſuch a Goad as one of theſe, that *Shamgar* made that prodigious ſlaughter related of him, *Judg.* 3. 31? I am confident that whoever ſhould ſee one of theſe Inſtruments, would judge it to be a Weapon, not leſs fit, perhaps fitter than a Sword for ſuch an Execution. Goads of this ſort I ſaw always us'd hereabouts, and alſo in *Syria*: and the reaſon is, becauſe the ſame ſingle Perſon both drives the Oxen, and alſo holds and manages the Plough; which makes it neceſſary to uſe ſuch a Goad as is above deſcrib'd, to avoid the encumbrance of two Inſtruments.

Friday, April 16.

Leaving *Kane Leban* we proceeded ſtill in our former Road; and paſſing by *Naploſa* and *Samaria*, we came to the Fountain *Selee*, and there took up our Lodging this night.

Saturday, April 17.

The next morning we continued on in the ſame Road that we travelled when outward bound, 'till we came to *Caphar Arab*. At this place we left our former way, and inſtead of turning off on the left hand to go for *Acra*, we kept our courſe ſtraight forwards, reſolving to croſs directly athwart the Plain of *Eſdraelon*, and to viſit *Nazareth*.

Proceeding in this courſe from *Caphar Arab*, we came in about half an hour to *Jeneen*. This is a large old Town, on the skirts of *Eſdraelon*: It has in it an old Caſtle, and two Moſques, and is the chief reſidence of the *Emir Chibly*. Here we were accoſted with a Command from the *Emir* not to advance any farther, 'till he ſhould come in perſon, to receive of us his Caphars. This was very unwelcome News to us, who had met with a tryal of his civility before. But however we had no remedy, and therefore thought it beſt to comply as contentedly as we could.

Having

Having been kept thus in ſuſpence from two in the morning 'till Sun ſet, we then received an order from the Prince, to pay the Caphar to an Officer, whom he ſent to receive it, and diſmiſs us.

Having receiv'd this Licence, we made all the haſte we could to diſpatch the Caphar, and to get clear of theſe Arabs, but notwithſtanding all our diligence, it was near midnight before we could finiſh. After which we departed, and entring immediately into the Plain of *Eſdraelon*, travell'd over it all night, and in ſeven hours reach'd its other ſide. Here we had a very ſteep and rocky aſcent; but however in half an hour we maſter'd it, and arriv'd at *Nazareth*.

Sunday, April 18.

Nazareth is at preſent only an inconſiderable Village, ſituate in a kind of round concave Valley, on the top of an high Hill. We were entertain'd at the Convent built over the place of the Annunciation. At this place are as it were immur'd, ſeven or eight Latin Fathers, who live a life truly mortified, being perpetually in fear of the Arabs, who are abſolute Lords of the Country.

We went in the afternoon to viſit the Sanctuary of this place. The Church of *Nazareth* ſtands in a Cave, ſuppos'd to be the place, where the Bleſſed Virgin receiv'd that joyful meſſage of the Angel, *Hail thou that art highly favoured*, &c. *Luke* 1. 28. It reſembles the figure of a Croſs. That part of it that ſtands for the Tree of the Croſs is fourteen paces long, and ſix over; and runs directly into the Grot, having no other Arch over it at top, but that of the natural Rock. The traverſe part of the Croſs is nine paces long and four broad, and is built athwart the Mouth of the Grot. Juſt at the ſection of the Croſs are erected two Granite Pillars, each two foot and one inch diameter, and about three foot diſtance from each other. They are ſuppos'd to ſtand on the very places, one, where the Angel, the other, where the Bleſſed Virgin ſtood at the time of the Annunciation. Of theſe Pillars, the innermoſt being that

that of the Blessed Virgin, has been broke away by the Turks, in expectation of finding Treasure under it; so that eighteen inches length of it is clean gone, between the Pillar and its Pedestal. Neverthelesś it remains erect; tho', by what art it is sustain'd, I could not discern. It touches the roof above, and is probably hang'd upon that: unless you had rather take the Fryars account of it, *viz.* that it is supported by a Miracle.

After this we went to see the House of *Joseph*, being the same, as they tell you, in which the Son of God liv'd, for near thirty years, in subjection to Man, *Luke* 2. 51. Not far distant from hence they shew you the Synagogue, where our Blessed Lord preach'd that Sermon, *Luke* 4. by which he so exasperated his Country-men. Both these places lie North West from the Convent, and were anciently dignified each with a handsom Church; but these Monuments of Queen *Helena*'s Piety are now in ruins.

Monday, April 19.

This day we destin'd for visiting *Mount Tabor*, standing by it self in the Plain of *Esdraelon*, about two or three furlongs within the Plain.

Its being situated in such a separate manner has induc'd most Authors to conclude, that this must needs be that holy Mountain (as St *Peter* styles it, 2 *Pet*. 1. 18.) which was the place of our Blessed Lord's Transfiguration, related *Mat*. 17. *Mark* 9. There you read that Christ *took with him* Peter, James *and* John *into a Mountain apart*; from which description they infer that the Mountain there spoke of can be no other than *Tabor*. The conclusion may possibly be true; but the argument us'd to prove it, seems incompetent; because the term κατ' ἰδίαν or *apart*, most likely relates to the withdrawing and retirement of the persons there spoken of; and not the situation of the Mountain.

After a very laborious ascent, which took up near an hour, we reach'd the highest part of the Mountain. It has a plain Area at top, most fertile and delicious, of an oval figure, extended about one furlong in breadth, and two in length. This Area is enclos'd with Trees on all parts, except toward the South. It was anciently invironed with Walls, and Trenches, and other Fortifications, of which it exhibits many remains at this day.

In this Area there are in ſeveral places, Ciſterns of good Water: But thoſe which are moſt devoutly viſited, are three contiguous Grottos made to repreſent the three Tabernacles which St *Peter* propos'd to erect, in the aſtoniſhment that poſſeſt him at the Glory of the Transfiguration. *Lord* (ſays he) *it is good for us to be here; let us make three Tabernacles, one for Thee,* &c.

I cannot forbear to mention in this place an obſervation, which is very obvious to all that viſit the *Holy-Land*, *viz.* that almoſt all Paſſages and Hiſtories related in the Goſpel are repreſented, by them that undertake to ſhew where every thing was done, as having been done moſt of them in Grottos; and that even in ſuch caſes, where the condition and circumſtances of the actions themſelves ſeem to require places of another nature.

Thus if you would ſee the place where St *Anne* was deliver'd of the Bleſſed Virgin, you are carried to a Grotto: If the place of the Annunciation, it is alſo a Grotto: If the place where the Bleſſed Virgin ſaluted *Elizabeth*; if that of the Baptiſt's, or that of our Bleſſed Saviour's Nativity; if that of the Agony, or that of St *Peter*'s Repentance, or that where the Apoſtles made the Creed, or this of the Transfiguration, all theſe places are alſo Grottos. And in a word, where-ever you go, you find almoſt every thing is repreſented as done under ground. Certainly Grottos were anciently held in great eſteem; or elſe they could never have been aſſign'd, in ſpight of all probability, for the places in which were done ſo many various Actions. Perhaps it was the Hermits way of living in Grottos from the fifth, or ſixth Century downward, that has brought them ever ſince to be in ſo great reputation.

From

Mount Tabor *Pag. 114.*

1 Naim. 2. Endor. 3. Mount Hermon. 4. The mountains of Gilboa. 5. The mountains of Samaria. 6. The river Kishon. 7. The Plain of Esdraelon. 8. valley of Iezrael.

From the top of *Tabor* you have a prospect, which, if nothing else, well rewards the labour of ascending it. It is impossible for Man's eyes to behold a higher gratification of this nature. On the North West you discern at a distance the Mediterranean; and all round you have the spacious and beautiful Plains of *Esdraelon* and *Galilee*, which present you with the view of so many places memorable for the resort and Miracles of the Son of God.

At the bottom of *Tabor* Westward stands *Daberah*, a small Village suppos'd by some to take its Name from *Deborah*, that famous Judge and Deliverer of *Israel*. Near this Valley is the Fountain of *Kishon*.

Not many leagues distant Eastward you see *Mount Hermon*; at the foot of which is seated *Nain*, famous for our Lord's raising the Widow's Son there, *Luke* 7. 14. and *Endor*, the place where dwelt the Witch consulted by *Saul*. Turning a little Southward you have in view the high Mountains of *Gilboah*, fatal to *Saul* and his Sons.

Due East you discover the Sea of *Tiberias*, distant about one day's Journey; and close by that Sea, they shew a steep Mountain, down which the Swine ran, and perish'd in the Waters. *Mat*. 8. 32.

A few points towards the North appears that which they call the *Mount of the Beatitudes*; a small rising, from which our Blessed Saviour deliver'd his Sermon in the 5, 6, 7 Chapters of St *Matthew*. Not far from this little Hill is the City *Saphet*, suppos'd to be the ancient *Bethulia*. It stands upon a very eminent and conspicuous Mountain, and is seen far and near. May we not suppose that Christ alludes to this City in those words of his Sermon, *Mat*. 5. 14. *A City set on a hill cannot be hid?* A conjecture which seems the more probable, because our Lord, in several places, affects to illustrate his discourse by comparisons taken from objects, that were then present before the eyes of his Auditors. As when he bids them, *behold the fowls of the air*, chap. 6. 16. *and the lilies of the field*, ibid, v. 28.

From *Mount Tabor* you have likewise the sight of a place, which they will tell you was *Dothaim*, where *Joseph* was sold by his Brethren; and of the Field, where our Blessed Saviour fed the Multitude with a few Loaves, and fewer Fishes. But whether it was the place where he divided the five Loaves and two Fishes amongst the five thousand, *Mat*. 14. 16. *&c*. or the seven Loaves amongst the four thousand, *Mat*. 15. 32. I left them to agree among themselves.

Having receiv'd great satisfaction in the sight of this Mountain, we return'd to the Convent the same way that we came. After dinner we made another small excursion, in order to see that which they call the *Mountain of the Precipitation*; that is, the brow of the Hill from which the *Nazarites* would have thrown down our Blessed Saviour, being incens'd at his Sermon preach'd to them, *Luke* 4. This Precipice is at least half a league distant from *Nazareth* Southward. In going to it you cross first over the Vale in which *Nazareth* stands; and then going down two or three furlongs in a narrow cleft between the Rocks, you there clamber up a short, but difficult way on the right hand; at the top of which, you find a great Stone standing on the brink of a Precipice, which is said to be the very place, where our Lord was destin'd to be thrown down by his enraged Neighbours, had he not made a miraculous escape out of their hands. There are in the Stone several little holes, resembling the prints of fingers thrust into it. These, if the Fryars say truth, are the impresses of Christ's fingers, made in the hard Stone, while he resisted the violence that was offer'd to him. At this place are seen two or three Cisterns for saving Water, and a few ruins; which is all that now remains of a Religious building founded here by the Empress *Helena*.

Tuesday, *April* 20.

The next morning we took our leaves of *Nazareth*, presenting the Guardian five a-piece, for his trouble and charge in entertaining us. We directed our course for *Acra*;

Acra; in order to which, going at first Northward, we cross'd the Hills that encompass'd the Vale of *Nazareth* on that side. After which we turn'd to the Westward, and pass'd in view of *Cana* of *Galilee*; the place signaliz'd with the beginning of Christ's Miracles, *John* 2. 11. In an hour and half more we came to *Sepharia*; a place reverenc'd for being the reputed habitation of *Joachim* and *Anna*, the Parents of the Blessed Virgin. It had once the Name of *Diocesaria*, and was a place in good repute: but at present it is reduced to a poor Village, shewing only here and there a few ruins, to testify its ancient better condition. On the West side of the Town stands good part of a large Church, built on the same place, where they say stood the House of *Joachim* and *Anna*; it is fifty paces long, and in breadth proportionable.

At *Sepharia* begins the delicious Plain of *Zabulon*. We were an hour and a half in crossing it; and, in an hour and a half more, passed by a desolate Village on the right hand, by Name *Satyra*. In half an hour more we enter'd the Plains of *Acra*, and in one hour and a half more arriv'd at that place. Our Stage this day was somewhat less than seven hours: It lay about West and by North, and thro' a Country very delightful, and fertile beyond imagination.

Wednesday, April 21.

At *Acra* we were very courteously treated by the French Consul and Merchant, as we had been when outward bound. Having staid only one night, we took our leaves; and returning by the same way of the Coast, that I have describ'd before, came the first night to our old Lodgings at *Solomon*'s Cisterns, and the second to *Sidon*.

Thursday, April 22.

Three hours distant from *Sidon*, we were carry'd by the French Consul to see a place, which we had passed by unregarded in our Journey outward; tho' it very well deserves a Traveller's Observation.

At

At about the diſtance of a Mile from the Sea, there runs along a high rocky Mountain; in the ſide of which are hewn a multitude of Grots, all very little differing from each other. They have entrances of about two foot ſquare. On the inſide you find, in moſt, or all of them, a Room of about four yards ſquare; On the one ſide of which is the door, on the other three, are as many little Cells, elevated about two foot above the floor. Here are of theſe ſubterraneous Caverns (as I was inform'd by thoſe who had counted them) two hundred in number. They go by the Name of the Grots of—— The great doubt concerning them is, whether they were made for the dead or the living. That which makes me doubt of this is, becauſe tho' all the ancient Sepulchers in this Country very much reſemble theſe Grottos; yet they have ſomething peculiar in them, which intices one to believe, they might be deſign'd for the reception of the living: For ſeveral of the Cells within were of a figure not fit for having Corpſes depoſited in them; being ſome a yard ſquare, ſome more, and ſome leſs; and ſeeming to be made for family uſes. Over the door of every Cell, there was a channel cut to convey the Water away, that it might not annoy the Rooms within. And becauſe the Cells were cut above each other, ſome higher, ſome lower, in the ſide of the Rock; here were convenient Stairs cut for the eaſier communication betwixt the upper and nether Regions. At the bottom of the Rock were alſo ſeveral old Ciſterns for ſtoring up Water. From all which arguments it may, with probability at leaſt, be concluded, that theſe places were contriv'd for the uſe of the living, and not of the dead. But what ſort of People they may be that inhabited this ſubterraneous City, or how long ago they liv'd, I am not able to reſolve. True it is, *Strabo* deſcribes the habitations of the *Troglodytæ* to have been ſomewhat of this kind.

Friday, *April* 23.

We continued this day at *Sidon*, being treated by our Friends of the French Nation with great generoſity.

Saturday,

Saturday, April 24.

This morning we took our leaves of the worthy French Consul, and the rest of our other Friends of that Nation, in order to go for *Damascus*.

Damascus lies near due East from *Sidon:* It is usually esteem'd three days Journey distant, the Road lying over the *Mountain Libanus* and *Anti-Libanus*.

Having gone about half an hour thro' the Olive yards of *Sidon*, we came to the foot of *Mount Libanus*. In two hours and a half more we came to a small Village called *Caphar Milki*. Thus far our ascent was easy; but now it began to grow more steep and difficult: In which having labour'd one hour and one third more, we then came to a fresh Fountain called *Ambus Lee*; where we encamp'd for this night. Our whole Stage was four hours and one third; Our Course East.

Sunday, April 25.

The next day we continued ascending for three good hours, and then arriv'd at the highest ridge of the Mountain, where the Snow lay close by the Road. We began immediately to descend again on the other side; and in two hours came to a small Village called *Meshgarah*, where there gushes out, at once, from the side of the Mountain, a plentiful Stream, which falling down into a Valley below, makes a fine Brook, and after a current of about two leagues, loses it self in a River called *Letane*.

At *Meshgarah* there is a * Caphar demanded by the Druses, who are the Possessors of these Mountains. We were for a little while perplex'd by the excessive demand made upon us by the Caphar-men; but finding us obstinate, they desisted.

Having gone one hour beyond *Meshgarah*, we got clear of the Mountain, and enter'd into a Valley called *Bocat*. This *Bocat* seems to be the same with *Bicath Aven*, mention'd *Amos* 1. 5. together with *Eden* and *Damascus*; for

* Half *per* Frank, quarter *per* Servant.

there

there is very near it, in Mount *Libanus*, a place call'd *Eden* to this day. It might also have the Name of *Aven*, that is, *Vanity* given it, from the Idolatrous Worship of *Baal*, practised at *Balbeck* or *Heliopolis*, which is situate in this Valley. The Valley is about two hours over, and in length extends several days Journey, lying near North East, and South West. It is enclosed on both sides with two parallel Mountains, exactly resembling each other; the one that which we lately pass'd over between this and *Sidon*, the other opposite against it towards *Damascus*. The former I take to be the true *Libanus*, the latter *Anti-Libanus*; which two Mountains are no where so well distinguish'd as at this Valley.

In the bottom of the Valley, there runs a large River called *Letane*. It rises about two days Journey Northward, not far from *Balbeck*; and keeping its course all down the Valley, falls at last into the River *Casimeer*, or (as it is erroneously called) *Eleutherus*.

Thus far our course had been due East; but here we inclin'd some points toward the North. Crossing obliquely over the Valley, we came in half an hour to a Bridge over the River *Letane*. It consists of five stone Arches, and is called *Kor A[illegible]en*, from a Village at a little distance, of the same Name. At this Bridge we cross'd the River, and having travell'd about an hour and a half on its bank, pitch'd our Tents there for this night. Our whole Stage was eight hours.

Monday, April 26.

The next morning we continued our oblique course over the Valley *Bocat*. In an hour we pass'd close by a small Village call'd *Jib Jeneen*, and in three quarters of an hour more, came to the foot of the Mountain *Anti-Libanus*. Here we had an easy ascent, and in half an hour pass'd by, on our right hand, a Village call'd *Uzzi*. In three quarters of an hour more we arriv'd at *Ayta*, a Village of Christians of the Greek Communion. At this last place the Road began to grow very rocky and trouble-

some;

some; in which having travell'd an hour, we arriv'd at a small Rivulet call'd *Ayn Tentloe*. Here we enter'd into a narrow cleft between two rocky Mountains, passing thro' which we arriv'd in four hours at *Demass*, gently descending all the way. At *Demass* a small * Caphar is demanded; which being dispatch'd, we put forward again, but had not gone above an hour and a half, when it grew dark, and we were forc'd to stop at a very inhospitable place, but the best we could find; affording no grass for our Horses, nor any water, but just enough to breed Frogs, by which we were serenaded all night.

Tuesday, April 27.

Early the next morning we deserted this uncomfortable Lodging, and in about an hour arriv'd at the River *Barrady*; our road still descending. This is the River that waters *Damascus*, and enriches it with all its plenty and pleasure. It is not so much as twenty yards over; but comes pouring down from the Mountains with great rapidity, and with so vast a Body of Water, that it abundantly supplies all the thirsty Gardens, and the City of *Damascus*.

We crossed *Barrady* at a new Bridge over it, called *Dummar*. On the other side our road ascended, and in half an hour, brought us to the brink of a high Precipice, at the bottom of which the River runs; the Mountain being here cleft asunder to give it admission into the Plain below.

At the highest part of the Precipice is erected a small Structure, like a Sheck's Sepulcher, concerning which the Turks relate this Story: That their Prophet, coming near *Damascus*, took his Station at that place for some time, in order to view the City; and considering the ravishing beauty and delightfulness of it, he would not tempt his frailty by entring into it; but instantly departed, with this reflection upon it, that there was but one Paradise design'd

* A quarter *per* Head.

for Man, and for his part he was resolv'd not to take His in this World.

You have indeed, from the Precipice, the most perfect prospect of *Damascus.* And certainly no place in the World can promise the Beholder, at a distance, greater voluptuousness. It is situate in an even Plain of so great extent, that you can but just discern the Mountains that compass it on the farther side. It stands on the West side of the Plain, at not above two miles distance from the place where the River *Barrady* breaks out from between the Mountains; its Gardens extending almost to the very place.

The City it self is of a long streight figure; its ends pointing near North East and South West. It is very slender in the middle, but swells bigger at each end, especially at that to the North East. In its length, as far as I could guess by my eye, it may extend near two miles. It is thick set with Mosques and Steeples, the usual ornaments of the Turkish Cities; and is encompass'd with Gardens, extending no less, according to common estimation, than thirty miles round; which makes it look like a noble City in a vast Wood. The Gardens are thick set with Fruit Trees of all kinds, kept fresh and verdant by the Waters of *Barrady.* You discover in them many Turrets, and Steeples, and Summer-Houses frequently peeping out from amongst the green Boughs, which may be conceiv'd to add no small advantage and beauty to the Prospect. On the North side of this vast Wood is a place call'd *Solhees,* where are the most beautiful Summer-Houses and Gardens.

The greatest part of this pleasantness and fertility proceeds, as I said, from the Waters of *Barrady,* which supply both the Gardens and City in great abundance. This River, as soon as it issues out from between the cleft of the Mountain before mention'd, into the Plain, is immediately divided into three Streams, of which, the middlemost and biggest runs directly to *Damascus* thro' a large open Field call'd, the *Ager Damascenus,* and is distributed to all the Cisterns and Fountains of the City. The other

two

two (which I take to be the work of Art) are drawn round, one to the right hand, and the other to the left, on the borders of the Gardens, into which they are let as they paſs, by little Currents, and ſo diſpers'd all over the vaſt Wood. Inſomuch that there is not a Garden, but has a fine quick Stream running thro' it; which ſerves not only for watering the place, but is alſo improved into Fountains, and other Water-works very delightful, tho' not contriv'd with that variety of exquiſite Art which is uſed in Chriſtendom.

Barrady being thus deſcrib'd, is almoſt wholly drunk up by the City and Gardens. What ſmall part of it eſcapes is united, as I was inform'd, in one Channel again, on the South Eaſt ſide of the City; and after about three or four hours courſe, finally loſes it ſelf in a Bog there, without ever arriving at the Sea.

The Greeks, and from them the Romans, call this river *Chryſorrhoas*. But as for *Abana* and *Pharpar*, rivers of *Damaſcus*, mention'd, 2 *Kings* 5. 12. I could find no memory, ſo much as of the Names remaining. They muſt doubtleſs have been only two Branches of the river *Barrady*; and one of them was probably the ſame Stream that now runs through the *Ager Damaſcenus*, directly to the City, which ſeems by its ſerpentine way to be a natural Channel: the other I know not well where to find; but it's no wonder, ſeeing they may and do turn, and alter the courſes of this river, according to their own convenience and pleaſure.

We continued a good while upon the Precipice, to take a view of the City; and indeed it is a hard matter to leave a Station which preſents you ſo charming a Landskip. It exhibits the Paradiſe below as a moſt fair and delectable place, and yet will hardly ſuffer you to ſtir away, to go to it: thus at once inviting you to the City, by the pleaſure which it ſeems to promiſe, and detaining you from it by the beauty of the Proſpect.

Coming down the Hill into the Plain, we were there met by a Janizary from the Convent, ſent to conduct us into the City. He did not think fit to carry us in at the West Gate, (which was nearest at hand) and so all across the City, to the Latin Convent where we were to lodge; for fear the *Damascens*, who are a very bigotted and insolent Race, should be offended at so great a number of Franks as we were: To avoid which danger, he led us round about the Gardens, before we arriv'd at the Gate. The Garden Walls are of a very singular Structure. They are built of great pieces of Earth, made in the fashion of Brick, and hardn'd in the Sun. In their dimensions they are two yards long each, and somewhat more than one broad, and half a yard thick. Two rows of these placed edge ways, one upon another, make a cheap, expeditious, and, in this dry Country, a durable Wall.

In passing between the Gardens, we also observ'd their method of scouring the Channels. They put a great bough of a Tree in the Water, and fasten to it a Yoke of Oxen. Upon the bough there sits a good weighty Fellow, to press it down to the bottom, and to drive the Oxen. In this equipage the bough is dragg'd all along the Channel, and serves at once both to cleanse the bottom, and also to mud and fatten the Water for the greater benefit of the Gardens.

Entring at the East Gate, we went immediately to the Convent, and were very courteously receiv'd by the Guardian, Father *Raphael*, a *Majorkine* by birth; and a Person who tho' he had dedicated himself to the contemplative Life, yet is not unfit for any affairs of the active.

Wednesday, April 28.

This morning we walk'd out to take a view of the City. The first place we went to visit, was the House of an eminent Turk. The Streets here are narrow, as is usual in hot Countries, and the Houses are all built, on the outside, of no better a material than either Sun-burnt Brick, or Flemish Wall, daub'd over in as course a manner as can be seen in the vilest Cottages. From this dirty way of building, they have this amongst other inconveniencies, that

that upon any violent Rain, the whole City becomes, by the washing of the Houses, as it were a Quagmire.

It may be wonder'd what should induce the People to build in this base manner, when they have in the adjacent Mountains such plenty of good Stone, for nobler Fabricks. I can give no reason for it, unless this may pass for such; that those who first planted here, finding so delicious a situation, were in haste to come to the enjoyment of it; and therefore nimbly set up those extemporary Habitations, being unwilling to defer their pleasure so long, as whilst they might erect more magnificent Structures: which primitive example their Successors have follow'd ever since.

But however in these mud Walls, you find the Gates and Doors adorn'd with Marble Portals, carv'd and inlaid with great beauty and variety. It is an object not a little surprizing, to see Mud and Marble, State and Sordidness so mingled together.

In the inside, the Houses discover a very different Face from what you see without. Here you find generally a large square Court, beautified with variety of fragrant Trees, and Marble Fountains, and compass'd round with splendid Apartments and Duans. The Duans are floor'd and adorn'd on the sides, with variety of Marble, mixt in Mosaick Knots and Mazes. The Ceilings and Traves are, after the Turkish manner, richly Painted and Guilded. They have generally Artificial Fountains springing up before them in Marble Basons; and, as for Carpets and Cushions, are furnish'd out to the height of Luxury. Of these Duans they have generally several on all sides of the Court, being plac'd at such different points, that at one or other of them, you may always have either the Shade or the Sun, which you please.

Such as I have describ'd was the House we went to see; and I was told the rest resemble the same description.

In the next place we went to see the Church of St. *John Baptist*, now converted into a Mosque, and held too sacred for Christians to enter, or almost to look into. However we had three short views of it, looking in at three

three ſeveral Gates. Its Gates are vaſtly large, and cover'd with Braſs, ſtampt all over with Arab Characters, and in ſeveral places with the figure of a Chalice, ſuppos'd to be the ancient Enſign or Arms of the Mamalukes. On the North ſide of the Church is a ſpacious Court, which I could not conjecture to be leſs than one hundred and fifty yards long, and eighty or one hundred broad. The Court is pav'd all over, and encloſed on the South ſide by the Church, on the other three ſides by a double Cloiſter, ſupported by two rows of Granite Pillars of the Corinthian Order, exceeding lofty and beautiful.

On the South ſide the Church joyns to the Bazars, and there we had an opportunity juſt to peep into it. It is within ſpacious and lofty, built with three Iſles, between which are rows of poliſh'd Pillars of a ſurprizing beauty; unleſs perhaps we were tempted to overvalue what was ſo ſparingly permitted to our Survey.

In this Church are kept the Head of St *John*, and ſome other Relicks eſteem'd ſo holy, that is is death even for a Turk to preſume to go into the Room, where they are kept. We were told here by a Turk of good faſhion, that Chriſt was to deſcend into this Moſque at the day of Judgment, as *Mahomet* was to do into that of *Jeruſalem*: but the ground and reaſon of this tradition, I could not learn.

From the Church we went to the Caſtle, which ſtands about two furlongs diſtant, towards the Weſt. It is a good Building of the ruſtick manner; in length it is three hundred and forty paces, and in breadth ſomewhat leſs. We were admitted but juſt within the Gate, where we ſaw ſtore of ancient Arms and Armour, the Spoils of the Chriſtians in former times. Amongſt the Artillery was an old Roman Baliſta; but this was a place not long to be gaz'd upon by ſuch as we were. At the Eaſt end of the Caſtle there hangs down in the middle of the Wall a ſhort Chain cut in Stone; of what uſe I know not, unleſs to boaſt the Skill of the Artificer.

Leaving this place we went to view the Bazars, which we found crowded with People, but deſtitute of any thing elſe worth obſerving.

Thurſday,

Thursday, April 29.

Very early this morning we went to see the yearly great Pomp of the Hadgees setting out on their Pilgrimage to *Mecca*; *Ostan*, Bassa of *Tripoli*, being appointed their Emir or Conductor for this year. For our better security from the insolencies of the over zealous votaries, we hired a Shop in one of the Bazars thro' which they were to pass.

In this famous Cavalcade there came first forty six Dellees, that is, Religious Madmen, carrying each a silk Streamer, mixt either of red and green, or of yellow and green; After these came three Troops of Segmen, an Order of Souldiers amongst the Turks; and next to them, some Troops of Spahees, another Order of Souldiery. These were follow'd by eight Companies of Mugrubines (so the Turks call the Barbaroses) on foot: These were Fellows of a very formidable aspect, and were design'd to be left in a Garrison, maintain'd by the Turks some where in the Desart of *Arabia*, and reliev'd every year with fresh Men. In the midst of the Mugrubines, there pass'd six small pieces of Ordinance. In the next place came on foot the Souldiers of the Castle of *Damascus*, fantastically Arm'd with Coats of Mail, Gauntlets, and other pieces of old Armour. These were follow'd by two troops of Janizaries, and their Aga, all mounted. Next were brought the Bassa's two Horse Tails, usher'd by his Aga of the Court; and next after the Tails follow'd six led Horses, all of excellent shape, and nobly furnish'd. Over the Saddle there was a Girt upon each led Horse, and a large Silver Target guilded with Gold.

After these Horses came the Mahmal. This is a large Pavilion of black Silk, pitch'd upon the back of a very great Camel, and spreading its Curtains all round about the Beast down to the ground. The Pavilion is adorn'd at top with a Gold Ball, and with Gold Fringes round about. The Camel that carries it wants not also his Ornaments of large Ropes of Beads, Fish-shells, Fox-tails, and other such fantastical finery hang'd upon his Head, Neck

and

and Legs. All this is design'd for the State of the Alcoran, which is placed with great reverence under the Pavilion, where it rides in State both to and from *Mecca*. The Alcoran is accompanied with a rich new Carpet which the Grand Signieur sends every year for the covering of Mahomet's Tomb, having the old one brought back in return for it, which is esteem'd of an inestimable value, after having been so long next Neighbour to the Prophet's rotten Bones. The Beast, which carries this sacred Load, has the privilege to be exempted from all other Burdens ever after.

After the Mahmal, came another Troop, and with them the Bassa himself; and last of all, twenty loaded Camels, with which the Train ended, having been three quarters of an hour in passing.

Having observ'd what we could of this Shew, (which perhaps was never seen by Franks before) we went to view some other Curiosities. The first place we came to was the *Ager Damascenus*, a long beautiful Meadow, just without the City, on the West side. It is divided in the middle by that branch of the river *Barrady* which supplies the City; and is taken notice of, because of a Tradition current here, that *Adam* was made of the Earth of this Field.

Adjoyning to the *Ager Damascenus* is a large Hospital: It has within it a pleasant square Court, enclos'd on the South side by a stately Mosque, and on its other sides with Cloisters, and Lodgings of no contemptible Structure.

Returning from hence homeward, we were shewn by the way a very beautiful Bagnio; and not far from it a Coffee-house capable of entertaining four or five hundred People, shaded over head with Trees, and with Matts when the Boughs fail. It had two Quarters for the reception of Guests; one proper for the Summer, the other for the Winter. That design'd for the Summer was a small Island, wash'd all round with a large swift Stream, and shaded over head with Matts and Trees. We found here a Multitude of Turks upon the Duans, regaling them-

themselves in this pleasant place; there being nothing which they behold with so much delight as Greens and Water: to which if a beautiful Face be added, they have a Proverb, that all three together make a perfect Antidote against Melancholy.

In the afternoon, we went to visit the House which, they say, was sometime the House of *Ananias*, the Restorer of sight to St. *Paul*, *Acts* 9. 17. The place shewn for it is (according to the old Rule) a small Grotto or Cellar, affording nothing remarkable, but only that there are in it a Christian Altar, and a Turkish praying place, seated nearer to each other, than well agrees with the nature of such places.

Our next Walk was out of the East Gate, in order to see the place (they say) of St. *Paul's* Vision, and what else is observable on that side. The place of the Vision is about half a Mile distant from the City, Eastward; It is close by the way side, and has no Building to distinguish it, nor do I believe it ever had: Only there is a small Rock or heap of Gravel which serves to point out the place.

About two furlongs nearer the City, is a small Timber Structure resembling the Cage of a Country Burrough. Within it is an Altar erected: there you are told, the holy Apostle rested for some time in his way to this City, after his Vision, *Acts* 9. 8.

Being return'd to the City, we were shewn the Gate at which St. *Paul* was let down in a Basket, *Acts* 9. 25. This Gate is at present wall'd up by reason of its vicinity to the East Gate, which renders it of little use.

Entring again into the City, we went to see the great Patriarch residing in this City. He was a Person of about forty years of Age. The place of his residence was mean, and his Person and Converse promis'd not any thing extraordinary. He told me there were more than one thousand two hundred Souls of the Greek Communion in that City.

Friday, April 30.

The next day we went to viſit the Gardens, and to ſpend a day there. The place where we diſpos'd of our ſelves was about a mile out of Town. It afforded us a very pleaſant Summer-houſe, having a plentiful Stream of Water running thro' it. The Garden was thick ſet with Fruit Trees, but without any Art or Order. Such as this, are all the Gardens hereabouts; only with this odds, that ſome of them have their Summer-houſes more ſplendid than others, and their Waters improv'd into greater variety of Fountains.

In viſiting theſe Gardens, Franks are oblig'd either to walk on foot, or elſe to ride upon Aſſes; the inſolence of the Turks not allowing them to mount on Horſeback. To ſerve them upon theſe occaſions, here are hackney Aſſes always ſtanding ready equipp'd for hire. When you are mounted, the Maſter of the Aſs follows his Beaſt to the place whether you are diſpos'd to go; goading him up behind with a ſharp pointed Stick, which makes him diſpatch his Stage with great Expedition. It is apt ſometimes to give a little diſguſt to the generous Traveller, to be forc'd to ſubmit to ſuch marks of ſcorn: but there is no remedy; and if the Traveller will take my advice, his beſt way will be to mount his Aſs contentedly, and to turn the Affront into a motive of Recreation, as we did. Having ſpent the day in the Garden, we return'd in the evening to the Convent.

Saturday, May 1.

The next day we ſpent at another Garden, not far diſtant from the former; but far exceeding it in the beauty of its Summer-houſe, and the variety of its Fountains.

Sunday, May 2.

We went, as many of us as were diſpos'd, to *Sydonaiia*, a Greek Convent about four hours diſtant from *Damaſcus*, to the Northward, or North by Eaſt: The Road, excepting

ing only two ſteep aſcents, is very good. In this Stage we paſs'd by two Villages, the firſt call'd *Tall*, the ſecond *Meneen*. At a good diſtance on the right hand is a very high Hill, reported to be the ſame on which *Cain* and *Abel* offer'd their Sacrifices; and where alſo the former ſlew his Brother, ſetting the firſt example of Blood-ſhed to the World.

Sydonaiia is ſituated at the farther ſide of a large Vale on the top of a Rock. The Rock is cut with Steps all up, without which it would be inacceſſible. It is fenced all round at the top, with a ſtrong Wall, which encloſes the Convent. It is a place of very mean Structure, and contains nothing in it extraordinary, but only the Wine made here, which is indeed moſt excellent. This place was at firſt Founded and Endow'd by the Emperor *Juſtinian*. It is at preſent poſſeſt by twenty Greek Monks, and forty Nuns, who ſeem to live promiſcuouſly together, without any order or ſeparation.

Here are upon this Rock, and within a little compaſs round about it, no leſs than ſixteen Churches or Oratories, Dedicated to ſeveral Names. The firſt, to St. *John*; ſecond, to St. *Paul*; third, to St. *Thomas*; fourth, to St. *Babylas*; fifth, to St. *Barbara*; ſixth, to St. *Chriſtopher*; ſeventh, to St. *Joſeph*; eighth, to St. *Lazarus*; ninth, to the *Bleſſed Virgin*; tenth, to St. *Demetrius*; eleventh, to St. *Saba*; twelfth, to St. *Peter*; thirteenth, to St. *George*; fourteenth, to *All Saints*; fifteenth, to the *Aſcenſion*; ſixteenth, to the *Transfiguration of our Lord*: From all which, we may well conclude, this place was held anciently in no ſmall repute for Sanctity. Many of theſe Churches I actually viſited; but found them ſo ruin'd and deſolate, that I had not courage to go to all.

In the Chappel, made uſe of by the Convent for their daily Services, they pretend to ſhew a great Miracle, done here ſome years ſince; of which take this Account, as I receiv'd it from them.

They had once in the Church a little Picture of the Bleſſed Virgin, very much reſorted to by Supplicants, and famous for the many Cures and Bleſſings granted in return to their Prayers. It happen'd that a certain Sacrilegious Rogue took an opportunity to ſteal away this Miraculous Picture: But he had not kept it long in his cuſtody, when he found it metamorphoſed into a real Body of Fleſh. Being ſtruck with wonder and remorſe at ſo prodigious an event, he carried back the prize to its true Owners, confeſſing and imploring forgiveneſs for his crime. The Monks having recover'd ſo great a Jewel, and being willing to prevent ſuch another diſaſter for the future, thought fit to depoſite it in a ſmall Cheſt of Stone; and placing it in a little Cavity in the Wall behind the high Altar, fixt an Iron Grate before it, in order to ſecure it from any fraudulent attempts for the future. Upon the Grates there are hang'd abundance of little toys and trinkets, being the offerings of many Votaries in return for the ſucceſs given to their Prayers at this Shrine. Under the ſame Cheſt, in which the Incarnate Picture was depoſited, they always place a ſmall Silver Baſon, in order to receive the diſtillation of an holy Oyl, which they pretend iſſues out from the encloſ'd Image, and does wonderful Cures in many Diſtempers, eſpecially thoſe affecting the Eyes.

On the Eaſt ſide of the Rock is an ancient Sepulcher hollow'd in the firm Stone. The Room is about eight yards ſquare, and contains in its ſides (as I remember) twelve Cheſts for Corpſes. Over the entrance there are carv'd ſix Statues as big as the Life, ſtanding in three Niches, two in each Nich. At the Pedeſtals of the Statues may be obſerv'd a few Greek words, which, as far as I was able to diſcern them in their preſent obſcurity, are as follows.

ΕΤΟΥϹΙΦ--	Ι[ΟΥ]Λ Δ ΦΙ[ΛΙ	ΙΟΥΛ Δ ΔΗΜΗ
ΙΟΥΛ Υ ΑΡΤЄ	Π] ΠΙΚΟϹ	ΤΡΙΟϹ ΚΑ[Ι Α[ΡΙ]
ШΙΔΙΡΟϹ ΚΑΙ	[Κ]ΑΙ ΔΟΜΝϹΙΝΑ	ΑΔΝΗ ΓΥ[ΝΗ]
ΠΡЄΙΓΚΥ ΓΥΝΗ	ΓΥΝΗ	ΠΑΝΤΑϹ ЄΠΟΙΟΥ[Ν]
Under the firſt.	*Under the ſecond.*	*Under the third Nich.*

A Gen-

A Gentleman in our Company, and my self have reason to remember this place, for an escape we had in it. A drunken Janizary, passing under the Window where we were, chanc'd to have a drop of Wine thrown out upon his Vest. Upon which innocent provocation, he presented his Pistol at us in at the Window: Had it gone off, it must have been fatal to one or both of us, who sate next the place. But it pleas'd God to restrain his fury. This evening we return'd again to *Damascus*.

Monday, May 3.

This morning we went to see the Street call'd *Straight, Acts* 9. 11. It is about half a mile in length, running from East to West thro' the City. It being narrow, and the Houses jutting out in several places on both sides, you cannot have a clear prospect of its length and straightness. In this Street is shewn the House of *Judas*, with whom St. *Paul* lodged; and in the same House is an old Tomb, said to be *Ananias*'s: but how he should come to be buried here, they could not tell us, nor could we guess; his own House being shewn us in another place. However the Turks have a reverence for this Tomb, and maintain a Lamp always burning over it.

In the afternoon, having presented the Convent with ten *per* Man for our kind reception, we took our leaves of *Damascus*, and shap'd our course for *Tripoli*; designing in the way to see *Balbeck*, and the Cedars of *Libanus*. In order to this, we return'd the same way by which we came; and crossing the river *Barrady* again at the Bridge of *Dummar*, came to a Village of the same Name a little farther, and there lodg'd this night. We travell'd this afternoon three hours.

Tuesday, May 4.

This morning we left our old Road, and took another more Northerly. In an hour and a half we came to a small Village call'd *Sinie*; just by which, is an ancient Structure on the top of an high Hill, suppos'd to be the Tomb

Tomb of *Abel*, and to have given the adjacent Country in old times the Name of *Abilene*. The Fratricide also is said by some to have been committed in this place. The Tomb is thirty yards long; and yet it is here believ'd to have been but just proportion'd to the Stature of Him who was buried in it. Here we enter'd into a narrow Gut, between two steep rocky Mountains, the river *Barrady* running at the bottom. On the other side of the river were several tall Pillars, which excited our Curiosity, to go and take a nearer view of them. We found them part of the front of some ancient, and very magnificent Edifice, but of what kind we could not conjecture.

We continued upon the Banks of *Barrady*, and came in three hours to a Village call'd *Maday*; and in two hours more to a Fountain call'd *Ayn il Hawra*, where we lodg'd. Our whole Stage was somewhat less than seven hours; our Course near North West.

Wednesday, May 5.

This morning we pass'd by the Fountain of *Barrady*, and came in an hour and two thirds to a Village call'd *Surgawich*. At this place, we left the narrow Valley, in which we had travelled ever since the morning before, and ascended the Mountain on the left hand. Having spent in crossing it, two hours, we arrived a second time in the Valley of *Bocat*; here steering Northerly directly up the Valley, we arrived in three hours at *Balbeck*. Our Stage this day was near seven hours, and our Course near about West.

At *Balbeck* we pitch'd at a place less than half a mile distant from the Town, Eastward, near a plentiful and delicious Fountain, which grows immediately into a Brook; and running down to *Balbeck*, adds no small pleasure and convenience to the place.

In the afternoon we walked out to see the City. But we thought fit, before we enter'd, to get License of the Governour, and to proceed with all caution. Being taught this necessary care by the example of some worthy English Gentlemen

The Prospect of Balbeck

Pag. 135

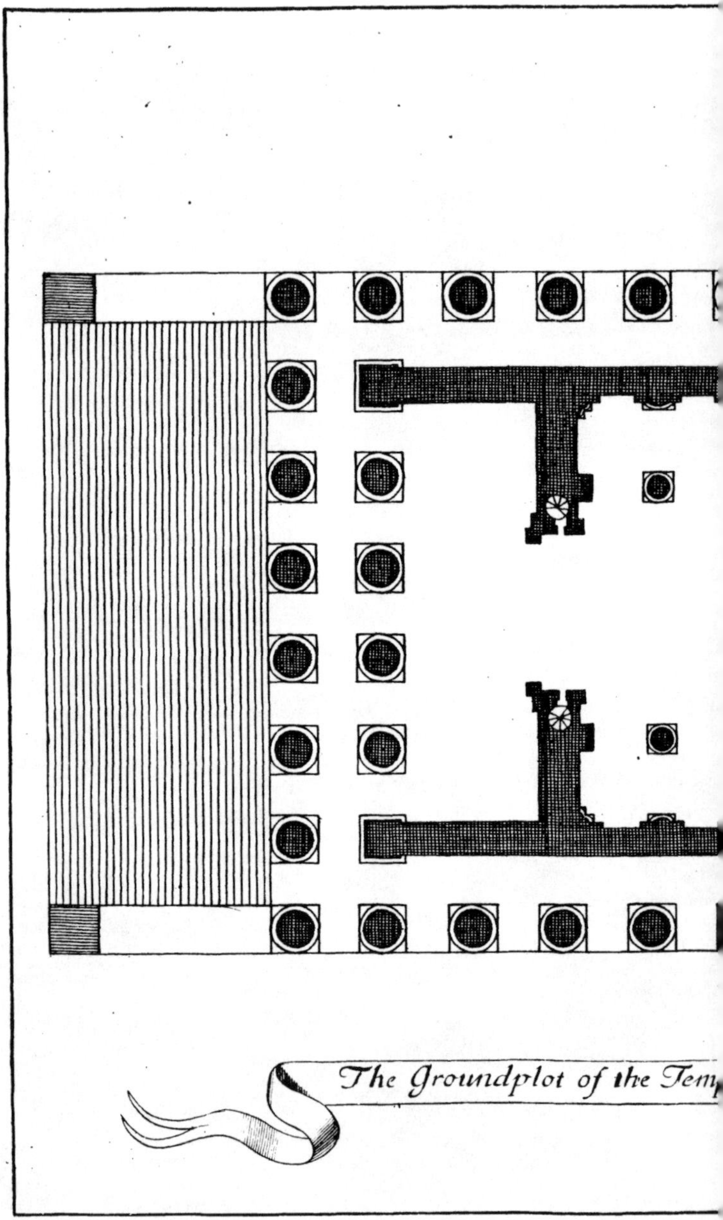

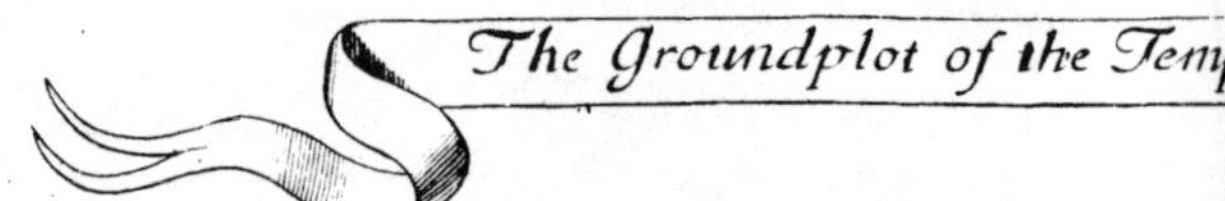
The Groundplot of the Tem

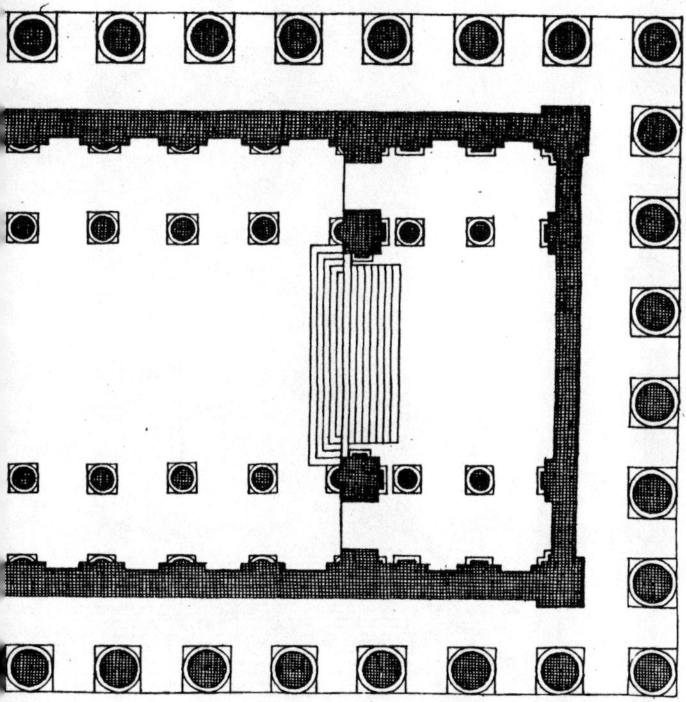

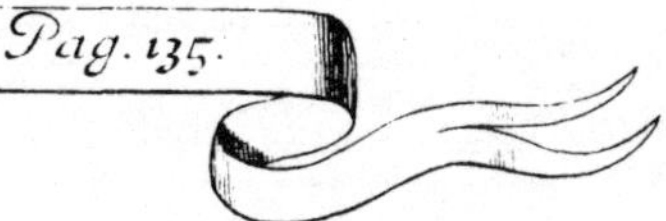

Balbeck. Pag. 135.

The Temple at
1
2
3
4
5
6

eck. Pag 135.
MBurghers sculp.

Hawksmor Inventor.

Balbeck Temple 135.
70 80 90 100 110 120
MBurghers delin et sculpsit

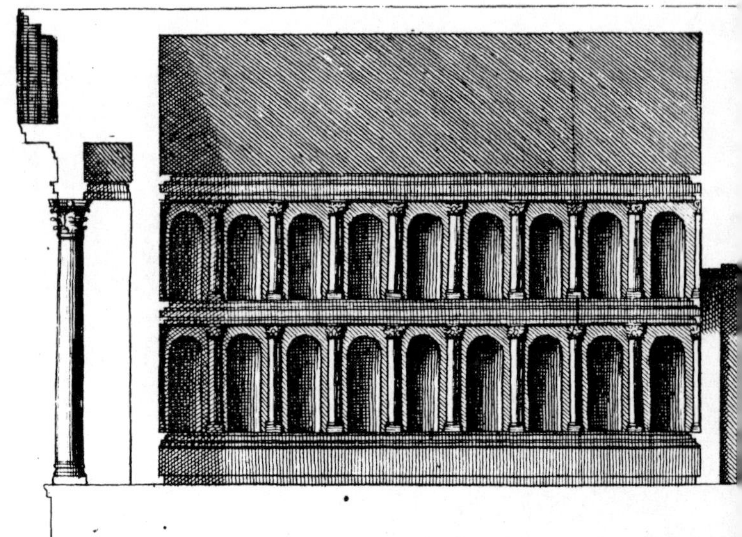

The Inward ſide of Balbeck T

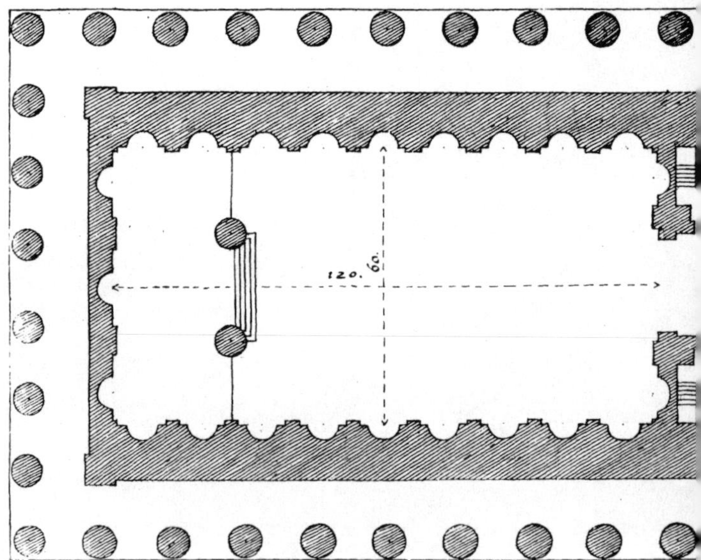

The Plan of the Temple at Bal

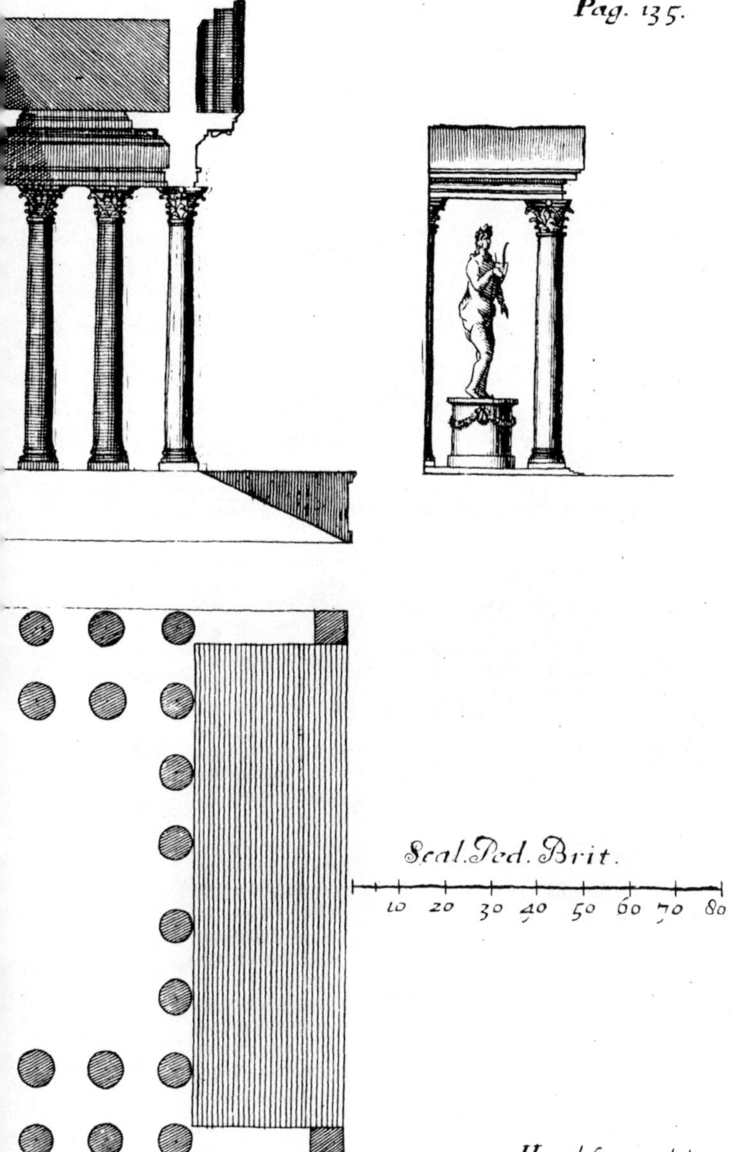

Scal. Ped. Brit.
10 20 30 40 50 60 70 80
Hawksmoor delin.
Burghers sculp.

The Front of the Temple at Balbeck.

Hawksmoor delin.
Burghers sculp.

The Inside of Balbeck Temple.

The Outward ſide of the Temple at Covent Garden.

The Tuſcan Temple in Covent Garden, Compard upon y^{e} ſame ſcale wth y^{e} Temple of Balbeck.

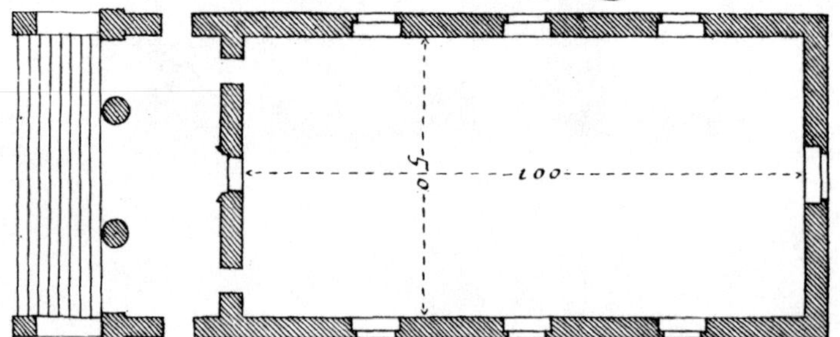

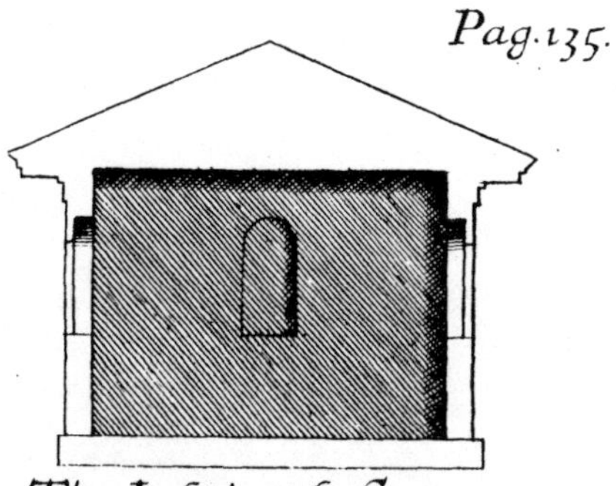

The Inside of Covent Garden Temple.

The Front of the Temple at Covent Garden.
B. Two Pilasters.

Hawksmoor delin.
Burghers sculp.

Gentlemen of our Factory; who visiting this place in the year 1689, in their return from *Jerusalem*, and suspecting no mischief, were basely intrigu'd by the People here, and forc'd to redeem their Lives at a great Sum of Money.

Balbeck is suppos'd to be the ancient *Heliopolis*, or *City of the Sun*; for that the word imports. Its present *Arab*, which is perhaps its most ancient Name, inclines to the same importance. For *Baal*, tho' it imports all Idols in general; of whatsoever Sex or Condition; yet it is very often appropriated to the Sun, the Sovereign Idol of this Country.

The City enjoys a most delightful and commodious situation, on the East side of the Valley of *Bocat*. It is of a square figure, compass'd with a tolerable good Wall, in which are Towers all round at equal distances. It extends, as far as I could guess by the eye, about two furlongs on a side. Its Houses within are all of the meanest Structure, such as are usually seen in Turkish Villages.

At the South West side of the City is a noble Ruin, being the only Curiosity for which this place is wont to be visited. It was anciently a Heathen Temple; together with some other Edifices belonging to it, all truly Magnificent: But in latter times these ancient Structures have been patch'd, and piec'd up with several other Buildings, converting the whole into a Castle, under which Name it goes at this day. The adjectitious Buildings are of no mean Architecture, but yet easily distinguishable from what is more ancient.

Coming near these Ruins, the first thing you meet with is a little round Pile of Building, all of Marble. It is encircled with Columns of the Corinthian Order, very beautiful, which support a Cornish that runs all round the Structure of no ordinary state and beauty. This part of it that remains, is at present in a very tottering condition, but yet the Greeks use it for a Church: and 'twere well if the danger of its falling, which perpetually threatens, would excite those People to use a little more fervour in their Prayers, than they generally do; the Greeks being seem-

ſeemingly the moſt undevout and negligent at their Divine Service, of any ſort of People in the Chriſtian World.

From this Ruin you come to a large firm pile of Building, which tho' very lofty, and compos'd of huge ſquare Stones, yet, I take to be part of the adjectitious work; for one ſees in the inſide ſome fragments of Images in the Walls and Stones, with Roman Letters upon them, ſet the wrong way. In one Stone we found graven DIVIS. and in another Line, MOSC. Thro' this pile you paſs in a ſtately arch'd Walk or Portico, one hundred and fifty paces long, which leads you to the Temple.

The Temple is an oblong ſquare, in breadth thirty two yards, and in length ſixty four, of which eighteen were taken up by the Πρόναος or Anti-Temple; which is now tumbled down, the Pillars being broke that ſuſtain'd it. The Body of the Temple, which now ſtands, is encompaſſed with a noble Portico, ſupported by Pillars of the Corinthian Order, meaſuring ſix foot and three inches in diameter, and about forty five foot in height, conſiſting all of three Stones a piece. The diſtance of the Pillars from each other, and from the Wall of the Temple, is nine foot. Of theſe Pillars there are fourteen on each ſide of the Temple, and eight at the end, counting the corner Pillars in both numbers.

On the Capitals of the Pillars there runs all round a ſtately Architrave, and Corniſh rarely carv'd. The Portico is cover'd with large Stones hollow'd Arch-wiſe, extending between the Columns, and the Wall of the Temple. In the Center of each ſtone is carv'd the figure of ſome one or other of the Heathen Gods, or Goddeſſes, or Heroes. I remember amongſt the reſt a *Ganymede*, and the Eagle flying away with him, ſo lively done that it excellently repreſented the ſenſe of that Verſe in *Martial*,

Illæſum timidis unguibus hæſit onus.

The Gate of the Temple is twenty one foot wide; but how high, could not be meaſur'd, it being in part fill'd up with rubbiſh. It is molded and beautified all round with exquiſite

exquisite Sculpture. On the nethermost side of the Portal, is carv'd a Fame hovering over the head as you enter, and extending its Wings two thirds of the breadth of the Gate; and on each side of the Eagle is describ'd a Fame likewise upon the Wing. The Eagle carries in its Pounces a *Caduceus*, and in his Beak the Strings or Ribbons coming from the ends of two *Festoons*; whose other ends are held and supported on each side, by the two Fames. The whole seem'd to be a piece of admirable Sculpture.

The measure of the Temple within, is forty yards in length, and twenty in breadth. In its Walls all round are two rows of Pilasters, one above the other; and between the Pilasters are Niches, which seem to have been design'd for the reception of Idols. Of these Pilasters, there are eight in a row, on each side; and of the Niches, nine.

About eight yards distance from the upper end of the Temple, stands part of two fine channell'd Pillars; which seem to have made a partition in that place, and to have supported a Canopy over the Throne of the chief Idol, whose Station appears to have been in a large Nich at this end. On that part of the partition which remains, are to be seen Carvings in Relievo representing Neptune, Tritons, Fishes, Sea-Gods, Arion and his Dolphin, and other Marine Figures. The covering of the whole Fabrick is totally broken down, but yet this I must say of the whole, as it now stands, that it strikes the Mind with an Air of Greatness beyond any thing that I ever saw before, and is an eminent proof of the Magnificence of the ancient Architecture.

About fifty yards distant from the Temple, is a row of Corinthian Pillars, very great and lofty; with a most stately Architrave and Cornish at top. This speaks it self to have been part of some very August Pile, but what one now sees of it is but just enough to give a regret, that there should be no more of it remaining.

Here is another Curiosity of this place, which a Man had need be well assur'd of his Credit, before he ventures to relate, lest he should be thought to strain the privilege

S of

of a Traveller too far. That which I mean is a large piece of the old Wall, or Περίβολος, which encompaſs'd all theſe Structures laſt deſcrib'd. A Wall made of ſuch monſtrous great Stones, that the Natives hereabouts (as it is uſual in things of this ſtrange Nature) aſcribe it to the Architecture of the Devil. Three of the Stones, which were larger than the reſt, we took the pains to meaſure, and found them to extend ſixty one yards in length; one twenty one, the other two each twenty yards. In deepneſs they were four yards each, and in breadth of the ſame dimenſion. Theſe three Stones lay in one and the ſame row, end to end. The reſt of the Wall was made alſo of great Stones, but none, I think, ſo great as theſe. That which added to the wonder was, that theſe Stones were lifted up into the Wall, more than twenty foot from the ground.

In the ſide of a ſmall aſcent, on the Eaſt part of the Town, ſtood an old ſingle Column, of the Tuſcan Order, about eighteen or nineteen yards high, and one yard and a half in diameter. It had a Channel cut in its ſide from the bottom to the top; from whence we judg'd it might have been erected for the ſake of raiſing Water.

At our return to our Tents, we were a little perplex'd by the Servants of the Moſolem, about our Caphar. We were contented at laſt to judge it at ten *per* Frank, and five *per* Servant, rather than we would engage in a long diſpute at ſuch a place as this.

Near the place where we were lodged was an old Moſque, and (as I ſaid before) a fine Fountain. This latter had been anciently beautified with ſome handſom Stone-work round it, which was now almoſt ruined; however it afforded us this imperfect Inſcription.

ΤΩΝ

ΤΩΝ ΧΕΙΜΕΡΕΙΩΝ Π≡≡ΟΝΕΩΚΤΙC ΤΟCΠΑΝΝ
ΒΛΕΠΕΙΝ ΔΕΔΩΚΕΝ ΩΡΡΕCΤΕΚΑΙ ΝΕΟΝ
ΧΡΥCΟΝ ΠΑΡΑCΧC≡CΩCΙ ΒΙΟC ΤΕ ΜΕΓΑC
ΥΔΩΡΤΕΝΥΝ=ΡΕCΤΙΠΗΓΑΙΟΝ ΠΟΛΥ
ΕΥΧΑΙC ΘΕΟΔΟΤΟΥΤΟΥ ΟCΙΟΥ ΕΠΙCΚΟΠΟΥ.

Thursday, May 6.

Early this morning we departed from *Balbeck*, directing our Course ſtraight acroſs the Valley. As we paſs'd by the Walls of the City, we obſerv'd many Stones Inſcrib'd with Roman Letters and Names; but all confus'd, and ſome placed upſide down: which demonſtrates that the Materials of the Walls were the Ruins of the ancient City.

In one place we found theſe Letters RMIPTITVEPR, in others theſe VARI---, in another NERIS, in others LVCIL--- and SEVERI and CELNAE and FIRMI; all which ſerve only to denote the reſort which the Romans had to this place in ancient times.

In one hour we paſs'd by a Village call'd *Te ad*; and in an hour more went to ſee an old Monumental Pillar, a little on the right hand of the Road. It was nineteen yards high, and five foot in diameter, of the Corinthian Order. It had a Table for an Inſcription on its North ſide, but the Letters are now perfectly eras'd. In one hour more, we reach'd the other ſide of the Valley, at the foot of Mount *Anti-Libanus*.

We immediately aſcended the Mountain, and in two hours came to a large Cavity between the Hills, at the bottom of which was a Lake call'd by its old Greek Name, *Limone*. It is about three furlongs over, and derives its Waters from the melting of the Snow. By this Lake our Guides would have had us ſtaid all night; aſſuring us that if we went up higher in the Mountains, we ſhould be forc'd to lie amongſt the Snow: but we ventur'd that, preferring a cold Lodging, before an unwholſome one. Having aſcended one hour, we arriv'd at the Snow; and proceeding amongst it for one hour and a half more, we then chose out as warm a place as we could find in so high a Region; and there we lodg'd this night upon the very top of *Libanus.* Our whole Stage this day was seven hours and a half.

Libanus is in this part free from Rocks, and only rises and falls with small, easy unevennesses, for several hours riding; but is perfectly barren and desolate. The ground, where not conceal'd by the Snow, appear'd to be cover'd with a sort of white Slates thin and smooth. The chief benefit it serves for, is, that by its exceeding height, it proves a conservatory for abundance of Snow, which thawing in the heat of Summer affords supplies of Water to the Rivers and Fountains in the Valleys below. We saw in the Snow, prints of the Feet of several wild Beasts, which are the sole Proprietors of these upper parts of the Mountains.

Friday, May 7.

The next morning we went four hours almost perpetually upon deep Snow; which, being frozen, bore us and our Horses: and then descending for about one hour, came to a Fountain call'd, from the Name of an adjacent Village, *Ayn il Hadede.* By this time we were got into a milder and better Region.

Here was the place, where we were to strike out of the way, in order to go to *Canobine* and the *Cedars.* And some of us went upon this design, whilst the rest chose rather to go directly for *Tripoli,* to which we had not now above four hours. We took with us a Guide, who pretended to be well acquainted with the way to *Canobine*; but he prov'd an ignorant Director: and after he had led us about for several hours in intricate and untrodden Mazes amongst the Mountains, finding him perfectly at a loss, we were forc'd to forsake our intended visit for the present, and to steer directly for *Tripoli*; where we arriv'd late at night, and were again entertain'd by our worthy Friends

Friends, Mr. *Consul Hastings* and Mr. *Fisher*, with their wonted friendship and generosity.

Saturday, *May* 8.

In the afternoon Mr. *Consul Hastings* carry'd us to see the Castle of *Tripoli*. It is pleasantly situate on a Hill, commanding the City; but has neither Arms, nor Ammunition in it, and serves rather for a Prison than a Garrison. There was shut up in it at this time a poor Christian Prisoner, call'd *Sheck Eunice*, a Maronite. He was one that had formerly renounc'd his Faith, and liv'd for many years in the Mahometan Religion: but in his declining Age, he both retracted his Apostacy, and dyed to attone for it; for he was impal'd by order of the Bassa two days after we left *Tripoli*. This punishment of impaling is commonly executed amongst the Turks for crimes of the highest degree; and is certainly one of the greatest indignities and barbarities that can be offered to human Nature. The execution is done in this manner. They take a Post of about the bigness of a Man's Leg, and eight or nine foot long, and make it very sharp at one end. This they lay upon the back of the Criminal, and force him to carry it to the place of Execution: imitating herein the old Roman Custom, of compelling Malefactors to bear their Cross. Being arriv'd at the fatal place, they thrust in the Stake at the Fundament of the Person, who is the miserable Subject of this doom; and then taking him by the Legs draw on his Body upon it, 'till the point of the Stake appears at his Shoulders. After this they erect the Stake, and fasten it in a hole dug in the ground. The Criminal sitting in this posture upon it, remains not only still alive, but also drinks, smokes, and talks, as one perfectly sensible; and thus some have continued for twenty four hours. But generally after the tortur'd Wretch has remain'd in this deplorable and ignominious posture an hour or two, some one of the Standers by is permitted to give him a gracious stab to the Heart; so putting an end to his unexpressible misery.

Sunday,

Sunday, May 9.

Despairing of any other opportunity, I made another attempt this day to see the *Cedars* and *Canobine*. Having gone for three hours across the Plain of *Tripoli*, I arriv'd at the foot of *Libanus*; and from thence continually ascending, not without great fatigue, came in four hours and a half to a small Village call'd *Eden*, and in two hours and a half more to the *Cedars*.

These noble Trees grow amongst the Snow near the highest part of *Lebanon*; and are remarkable as well for their own age and largeness, as for those frequent allusions made to them in the Word of God. Here are some of them very old, and of a prodigious bulk; and others younger of a smaller size. Of the former I could reckon up only sixteen; and the latter are very numerous. I measured one of the largest, and found it twelve yards six inches in girt, and yet sound; and thirty seven yards in the spread of its boughs. At about five or six yards from the ground, it was divided into five Limbs, each of which was equal to a great Tree.

After about half an hour spent in surveying this place, the Clouds began to thicken, and to fly along upon the ground; which so obscur'd the road, that my Guide was very much at a loss to find our way back again. We rambled about for seven hours thus bewildred, which gave me no small fear of being forc'd to spend one night more at *Libanus*. But at last, after a long exercise of pains and patience, we arriv'd at the way that goes down to *Canobine*; where I arriv'd by that time it was dark, and found a kind reception, answerable to the great need I had of it, after so long a fatigue.

Canobine is a Convent of the Maronites, and the Seat of the Patriarch, who is at present *F. Stephanus Edenensis*, a Person of great learning and humanity. It is a very mean Structure, but its situation is admirably adapted for Retirement and Devotion: for there is a very deep rupture in the side of *Libanus*, running at least seven hours travel directly

Religieus der Maroniten.
Pag. 163.

Patriarch der Maroniten.
Pag. 165.

directly up into the Mountain. It is on both ſides exceeding ſteep and high, cloath'd with fragrant Greens from top to bottom, and every where refreſh'd with Fountains, falling down from the Rocks in pleaſant Caſcades; the ingenious work of Nature. Theſe Streams, all uniting at the bottom, make a full and rapid Torrent, whoſe agreeable murmuring is heard all over the place, and adds no ſmall pleaſure to it. *Canobine* is ſeated on the North ſide of this Chaſm, on the ſteep of the Mountain, at about the midway between the top and the bottom. It ſtands at the mouth of a great Cave, having a few ſmall Rooms fronting outward, that enjoy the light of the Sun; the reſt are all under ground. It had for its Founder the Emperour *Theodoſius* the Great, and tho' it has been ſeveral times rebuilt, yet the Patriarch aſſur'd me, the Church was of the Primitive Foundation. But whoever built it, it is a mean Fabrick, and no great Credit to its Founder. It ſtands in the Grot, but fronting outwards receives a little light from that ſide. In the ſame ſide there were alſo hang'd in the Wall two ſmall Bells, to call the Monks to their Devotions: a privilege allow'd no where elſe in this Country; nor would they be ſuffer'd here, but that the Turks are far enough off from the hearing of them.

The Valley of *Canobine* was anciently (as it well deſerves) very much reſorted to for religious retirement. You ſee here ſtill Hermitages, Cells, Monaſteries, almoſt without number. There is not any little part of Rock, that jets out upon the ſide of the Mountain, but you generally ſee ſome little Structure upon it, for the reception of Monks and Hermits; tho' few or none of them are now Inhabited.

Monday, May 10.

After Dinner I took my leave of the Patriarch, and return'd to *Tripoli*. I ſteer'd my Courſe down by a narrow oblique Path, cut in the ſide of the rupture, and found it three hours before I got clear of the Mountain, and three more afterwards before I came to *Tripoli*.

Tueſday,

Tuesday, *May* 11.

This day we took our leaves of our worthy *Tripoli* Friends, in order to return for *Aleppo*. We had some debate with our selves, whether we should take the same way by which we came, when outward bound, or a new one by *Emissa Hempse* and *Hamal*. But we had notice of some disturbances upon this latter road; so we contented our selves to return by the same way we came: for having had enough by this time both of the pleasure, and of the fatigue of travelling, we were willing to put an end to both, the nearest and spediest way. All that occurr'd to us new, in these days Travel, was a particular way us'd by the Country People in gathering their Corn; it being now Harvest time. They pluck'd it up by handfuls from the roots; leaving the most fruitful Fields as naked as if nothing had ever grown on them. This was their practice in all places of the East that I have seen: and the reason is, that they may lose none of their Straw, which is generally very short, and necessary for the sustenance of their Cattle; no Hay being here made. I mention this, because it seems to give light to that expression of the *Psalmist*, *Ps.* 129. 6. *which withereth before it be plucked up*, where there seems to be a manifest allusion to this Custom. Our new Translation renders this place otherwise: but in so doing it differs from most, or all other Copies; and here we may truly say, *the old is the better.* There is indeed mention of a Mower in the next Verse; but then it is such a Mower as fills not his hand; which confirms rather than weakens the preceding Interpretation.

Returning therefore by our former Stages, without any notable alteration or occurrence, we came in eight days to the *Honey Kane*: at which place we found many of our *Aleppine* Friends, who having heard of our drawing homeward were come to meet us, and welcome us home. Having dined together, and congratulated each other upon our happy reunion, we went onward the same evening to *Aleppo*.

Thus

Thus, by God's infinite mercy and protection, we were restor'd all in safety to our respective Habitations. And here before I conclude, I cannot but take notice of one thing more, which I should earnestly recommend to the devout and grateful remembrance of every Person engag'd in this Pilgrimage: *viz.* that amongst so great a Company as we were, amidst such a multiplicity of dangers and casualties, such variety of Food, Airs and Lodgings (very often none of the best) there was no one of us that came to any ill accident throughout our whole Travels; and only one that fell Sick by the consequences of the Journey, after our return. Which I esteem the less diminution to so singular a mercy, in regard that amongst so many of my dear Friends and Fellow Travellers, it fell to my own share to be the Sufferer.

Δόξα Θεῷ.

F I N I S.

Since the Book was Printed off, the two following Letters, relating to the ſame Subject, were communicated by the Reverend Mr. Osborn *Fellow of* Exeter *College; to whom they were ſent by the Author, in Anſwer to ſome Queſtions propos'd by Him.*

SIR,

I Received yours of *June* 27. 1698. and return'd you an Anſwer to it in brief, about three Months ſince; promiſing to ſupply what was then wanting, at ſome other opportunity: which promiſe I ſhall now make good. You deſired an Account of the *Turks*, and of our way of living amongſt them. As to the former, it would fill a Volume to write my whole thoughts about them. I ſhall only tell you at preſent, that I think they are very far from agreeing with that Character which is given of them in Chriſtendom; eſpecially for their exact Juſtice, Veracity, and other moral Virtues: upon account of which, I have ſometimes heard them mention'd with very extravagant Commendations; as tho' they far exceeded Chriſtian Nations. But I muſt profeſs my ſelf of another Opinion: For the Chriſtian Religion, how much ſoever we live below the true Spirit and Excellency of it, muſt

ſtill

ſtill be allow'd to diſcover ſo much Power upon the minds of it's Profeſſors, as to raiſe them far above the level of a *Turkiſh* Virtue. 'Tis a Maxim that I have often heard from our Merchants, that a *Turk* will always cheat when he can find an opportunity. Friendſhip, Generoſity, and Wit (in the *Engliſh* Notion) and delightful Converſe, and all the Qualities of a refin'd and ingenuous Spirit, are perfect Strangers to their Minds; tho' in Traffick and Worldly Negotiations, they are acute enough: and are able to carry the Accounts of a large Commerce in their Heads, without the help of Books, by a natural Arithmetick, improv'd by Cuſtom and Neceſſity. Their Religion is fram'd to keep up great outward Gravity and Solemnity, without begetting the leaſt good tincture of Wiſdom or Virtue in the Mind. You ſhall have 'em at their hours of Prayer (which are four a day always) addreſſing themſelves to their Devotions with the moſt ſolemn and critical Waſhings, always in the moſt publick places, where moſt People are paſſing; with moſt lowly and moſt regular Proſtrations, and a hollow Tone; which are amongſt them the great Excellencies of Prayer. I have ſeen 'em in an affected Charity, give Money to Bird-catchers (who make a Trade of it) to reſtore the poor Captives to their natural Liberty; and at the ſame time hold their own Slaves in the heavieſt Bondage. And at other times they'll buy Fleſh to relieve indigent Dogs and Cats; and yet curſe you with Famine and Peſtilence, and all the moſt hideous Execrations: in which way theſe Eaſtern Nations have certainly the moſt exquiſite Rhetorick of any People upon Earth. They know hardly any Pleaſure but that of the ſixth Senſe. And yet with all this, they are incredibly conceited of their own Religion; and contemptuous of that of others: which I take to be the great Artifice of the Devil, in order to keep them his own. They are a perfect viſible Comment upon our Bleſſed Lord's Deſcription of the *Jewiſh* Phariſees. In a word, Luſt, Arrogance, Covetouſneſs, and the moſt exquiſite Hypocriſy compleat their Character. The only thing that ever I could obſerve to commend in them, is the outward Decency of their Carriage, the profound Reſpect they pay to Religion and to every thing relating to it, and their great Temperance and Frugality. The dearneſs of any thing is no motive in *Turky*, tho' it be in *England*, to bring it into Faſhion,

As for our living amongſt them, it is with all poſſible quiet and ſafety: And that's all we deſire, their Converſation being not in the leaſt entertaining. Our Delights are among our ſelves: and here being more than forty of Us, we never want a moſt Friendly and Pleaſant Converſation. Our way of Life reſembles, in ſome meaſure, the Academical. We live in ſeparate Squares, ſhut up every night after the manner of Colleges. We begin the day conſtantly, as You do, with Prayers; and have our ſet times for Buſineſs, Meals and Recreations. In the Winter we Hunt in the moſt delightful Campaign twice a week; and in the Summer go as often to divert

divert Our ſelves under Our Tents, with Bowling, and other Exerciſes. So that you ſee we want not Divertiſements; and theſe all Innocent and Manly. In ſhort, 'tis my real Opinion, that there is not a Society out of *England*, that for all good and deſireable Qualities, may be compar'd to this. But enough of this Confuſion, which I would have ſhorten'd, and put in better order, if I had had time.

March 10. 169$\frac{8}{9}$.

SIR,

SIR,

AS for your Queſtions about *Gehazi*'s Poſterity, and the Greek Excommunications, I have little to anſwer; but yet I hope enough to give You and your Friend ſatisfaction. When I was in the *Holy Land*, I ſaw ſeveral that labour'd under *Gehazi*'s Diſtemper; but none that could pretend to derive his Pedigree from that Perſon. Some of them were poor enough to be his Relations: particularly at *Sichem* (now *Naploſu*) there were no leſs than ten (the ſame number that was cleans'd by our *Saviour* not far from the ſame place) that came a begging to Us at one time. Their manner is to come with ſmall Buckets in their hands, to receive the Alms of the Charitable; their touch being ſtill held infectious, or at leaſt unclean. The Diſtemper, as I ſaw it in them, was very different from what I have ſeen it in *England*: for it not only defiles the whole ſurface of the Body with a foul Scurf; but alſo deforms the Joynts of the Body; particularly thoſe of the Wriſts and Ancles; making them ſwell with a Gouty ſcrofulous Subſtance, very loathſom to look upon. I thought their Legs reſembled thoſe of old batter'd Horſes, ſuch as are often ſeen in Drays in *England*. The whole Diſtemper indeed, as it there appear'd, was ſo ſo noiſome, that it might well paſs for the utmoſt Corruption of the Human Body on this ſide the Grave. And certainly the inſpired Pen-men could not have found out a fitter Emblem, whereby to expreſs the uncleanneſs and odiouſneſs of Vice. But to return to *Gehazi*: 'Tis no wonder if the deſcent from him be by time obſcur'd; ſeeing the beſt of the Jews, at this time of day, are at a loſs to make out their Genealogies. But beſides, I ſee no neceſſity in Scripture for his Line's being perpetuated. The term (*for Ever*) is, you know, often taken in a limited ſenſe in Holy-writ; of which the deſignation of *Phineas*'s Family to the Prieſthood, *Numb.* 25. 13. may ſerve for an Inſtance. His Poſterity was, you know, cut entirely off from the Prieſthood, and that transferr'd to *Eli* (who was one of another Line) about 300 years after.

I have enquired of a Greek Prieſt, a Man not deſtitute either of Senſe or Probity, about your other Queſtion. He poſitively affirmed it, and produced an Inſtance of his own Knowledge in Confirmation of it. He ſaid, that about 15 years ago, a certain Greek departed this Life without Abſolution; being under the guilt of a Crime, which involv'd him in the ſentence of Excommunication, but unknown to the Church. He had Chriſtian Burial given him; and about 10 years after, a Son of his dying, they had occaſion to open the ground near where his Body was laid, in order to bury his Son by him. By which means they diſcover'd his Body as entire, as when it was firſt laid in the Grave. The Shrowd was rotted

rotted away, and the Body naked and black, but perfectly ſound. Report of this being brought to the Biſhop, he immediately ſuſpected the cauſe of it; and ſent ſeveral Prieſts (of whom the Relator was one) to pray for the Soul of the departed, and to abſolve him at his Grave. Which they had no ſooner done, but (as the Relator goes on) the Body inſtantly diſſolv'd and fell into Duſt like ſlack'd Lime. And ſo (well ſatisfied with the Effect of their Abſolution) they departed. This was delivered to me *verbo Sacerdotis*. The Man had hard fortune not to dye in the Romiſh Communion; for then his Body being found ſo entire would have entitled him to Saintſhip. For the Romaniſts, as I have both heard and ſeen, are wont to find out and maintain the Relicks of Saints by this token. And the ſame ſign, which proves an *Anathema Maranatha* amongſt the Greeks, demonſtrates a Saint amongſt the Papiſts: perhaps both equally in the right.

April 12. 1700.

AN ACCOUNT OF THE AUTHOR'S JOURNEY FROM *Aleppo* to the River *Euphrates*, the City *Beer*, and to *Mesopotamia*.

WE set out from *Aleppo, April 17th 1699.* and steering East North East, somewhat less, we came in three hours and a half to *Surbass*.

Tuesday, April 18.

We came in three hours and a half to *Bezay*, passing by *Bab*, where is a good Aqueduct * *Dyn il Daab*, to which you descend by about thirty Steps; and *Lediff* a pleasant Village. Our Course thus far was East and by North. In the Afternoon we advanced three hours further, Course North East, to an old ruin'd Place, formerly of some Consideration, called *Acamy:* It is situated in the Wilderness on a Hill encompassed by a Valley; It was large, and had the footsteps of some Symmetry, good Walls and Buildings.

Wednesday, April 19.

We went East and by North, and in four hours arriv'd at *Bambych*. This Place has no remnants of its Ancient

* The District of *Daab*.

U Greatness,

Greatneſs, but its Walls, which may be traced all round, and cannot be leſs than three Miles in compaſs. Several fragments of them remain on the Eaſt Side, eſpecially at the Eaſt Gate; and another piece of eighty yards long, with Towers of large ſquare ſtone extreamly well built. On the North Side I found a Stone with the Buſts of a Man and Woman, large as the life; and under, two Eagles carv'd on it. Not far from it, on the ſide of a large Well, was fixed a Stone with three Figures carved on it, in Baſſo Relievo. They were two Syrens, which twining their fiſhy Tails together, made a Seat, on which was placed ſitting a naked Woman, her Arms and the Syrens on each ſide mutually entwined.

On the Weſt Side is a deep Pit of about 100 yards diameter. It was low, and had now Water in it, and ſeem'd to have had great Buildings all round it; with the Pillars and Ruins of which, it is now in part filled up; but not ſo much, but that there was ſtill Water in it. Here are a multitude of Subterraneous Aqueducts brought to this City; the People atteſted no fewer than fifty. You can ride no where about the City, without ſeeing them. We pitched by one about a quarter of a mile Eaſt of the City, which yields a fine Stream; and emptying it ſelf into a Valley, waters it, and makes it extreamly fruitful. Here perhaps were the Paſtures of the Beaſts deſign'd for Sacrifices. Here are now only a few poor Inhabitants, tho' anciently all the North Side was well inhabited by *Saracens*; as may be ſeen by the remains of a noble Moſque and a Bagnio a little without the Walls. We were here viſited by a Company of *Begdelies*, who were incamped ſome hours further towards *Euphrates*, having about 1000 Horſe there.

Thurſday, April 20.

For avoiding the *Begdelies*, we hired a Guide, who conducted us a by-way. We travelled *North North Eaſt*, over a deſert Ground; and came in three hours to a ſmall Rivulet called *Sejour*, which falls into the *Euphrates* about

about three hours below *Jerabolus.* In about two hours more we came to a fine fruitful Plain covered with extraordinary Corn, lying between the Hills and the River *Euphrates.* In about an hour and half's travelling thro' this Plain on the banks of the River, we came to *Jerabolus.* This place is of a ſemicircular figure, its flat ſide lying on the banks of *Euphrates*; on that ſide it has a high long Mount, cloſe by the water, very ſteep. It was anciently built upon; (and at one end of it, I ſaw fragments of) very large Pillars, a yard and half diameter, and Capitals and Corniſhes well carved. At the foot of the Mount was carved on a large ſtone a Beaſt reſembling a Lyon, with a bridle in his mouth; and I believe anciently a Perſon ſitting on it: but the ſtone is in that part now broke away; the Tail of the Beaſt was Couped.

Round about this place are high banks caſt up, and there is the footſteps of walls on them. The gates ſeem to have been well built: the whole was 2250 paces, that is yards, in circumference. The River is here as large as the *Thames* at *London*; a long bullet-gun could not ſhoot a ball over it, but it dropt into the water. Here is found a large Serpent which has legs and claws, call'd *Woralla.* I was told by a Turk, that a little below this place, when the River is low, may be ſeen the Ruins of a ſtone-bridge over the River: for my own part I ſaw it not, nor do I much rely on the Turks veracity. The River ſeem'd to be lately fallen very ſuddenly; for the banks were freſhly wet, two yards and more above the water. It was here North and South.

Friday, April 21.

We kept cloſe on the banks of *Euphrates*, and in two hours and a half croſſed a fine Rivulet called *Towzad*; and in two hours more arrived over againſt *Beer*, and pitched on a Flat, cloſe by the River ſide. Obſerving the Latitude of the place by my Quadrant, I found the Angle between the Sun and the Zenith to be twenty two

 degrees;

degrees; and the declination this Day being 15 degrees 10 minutes, the whole is 37 degrees 10 minutes.

Saturday, April 22.

We continued at our Station, not daring to croſs the River, for fear of falling into the hands of the *Chiah* of the *Baſhaw* of *Urfa*, who was then at *Beer* ordering many Boats of Corn down to *Bagdal*. We were ſupplyed at the ſame time with proviſions by *Sheck Aſſyne*, to whom we made returns.

Sunday, April 23.

The *Chiah* being now departed, *Sheck Aſſyne* invited us over to *Beer*: We croſſed in a Boat of the Country, of which they have a great many, this being the great Paſs into *Meſopotamia*. The Boats are of a miſerable Fabrick, flat and open in the fore part, for Horſes to enter: They are large enough to carry about four Horſes each. Their way to croſs is, by drawing up the Boat as high as they know to be neceſſary; and then with wretched Oars ſtriking over, ſhe falls a good way down by the force of the Stream, before they arrive at the further ſide.

Having ſaluted *Aſſyne*, we were conducted to ſee the Caſtle; which is a large old Building on the top of a great long Rock, ſeparated by a great gulph or natural bottom, from the land. At firſt coming within the Gates which are of Iron, we ſaw ſeveral large Globes of Stone about twenty inches diameter; and great Axles of Iron, with wheels, which were intire blocks of wood two foot thick in the Nave, and cut ſomewhat to an edge toward the Periphery; and Screws to bend Bows or Engines; as alſo ſeveral Braſs Field Pieces.

Aſcending up the ſides of the Rock by a way cut obliquely, you come to the Caſtle. At firſt entrance, you find a way cut under ground down to the River. In the Caſtle, the principal things we ſaw, were, firſt a large Room full of old Arms: I ſaw there Glaſs Bottles to be ſhot at the end of Arrows; one of them was ſtuck at the end

end of an Arrow, with four pieces of Tin by its ſides, to keep it firm. Vaſt large Croſs-bows, and Beams, ſeemingly deſign'd for Battering-Rams ; and Roman Saddles and Head pieces of a large ſize ; ſome of which were painted ; and ſome large Thongs for Bow-ſtrings and bags for ſlinging Stones. But the Jealouſy of the Turks would not permit us to ſtay ſo long, as would have been requiſite for a perfect examination of theſe Antiquities.

From the Caſtle we returned to *Aſſyne*, and were civilly treated. In the Evening we went up into the Country of *Meſopotamia*. The Hills are Chalky and Steep ; and come cloſe to the Water ſide without a Plain intervening, as it is upon the ſide of *Syria* ; ſo that *Beer* ſtands on the ſide of a Hill. However it has a couple of fine Streams that run over the Top of the Hill ; one of which drives two Mills, and ſo runs down to the City, which is well walled. In the ſide of the Hill, there is a *Kane* under ground cut into the Rock, with fifteen large Pillars left to ſupport its Roof.

Monday, April 24.

We left *Beer*, and travelling Weſt came in three hours to *Nizib*, a place well ſituated at the head of the *Towzad*. Here is an old ſmall Church, very ſtrong and intire ; only the Cupola in the middle of the croſs is broke down, and its ſpace covered with Leaves, to fit the place for a Moſque. I believe the Turks made the places to which they turn in Prayers, empty Niches, to ſhew that they worſhipped one Inviſible God not to be repreſented by Images. In two hours we came from *Nizib* to a good Chriſtian Village called *Uwur* ; and in an hour and half more, to a Well in the Deſart.

Tueſday, April 25.

We travelled Weſt near two hours ; and came through a fine Country diverſified into ſmall Hills and Valleys, to a Village called *Adjia*, having left *Silam* and two other Villages on the right hand. At *Adjia* riſes the River

River of *Aleppo*, from a large Fountain, at once; and just above it runs the *Sejour*, which might be let into it by a short cut of ten yards. From *Adjia*, our Course was West North West. The Banks of the *Sejour* are well planted with Trees and Villages. In two little hours we came to *Antab*, having crossed the *Sejour* at a Bridge, about three quarters of an hour before. Leaving the City on the Right hand, we passed under its Walls, and pitched about three quarters of an hour from it, on a plain Field on the Banks of the *Sejour*.

Antab stands mostly on a Hill, having a Castle on a Round Mount, at its North side, exactly resembling that of *Aleppo*, tho' much less. It has a very deep Ditch round it: and at the foot of the Mount within the Ditch, is a Gallery cut through the Rock all round the Castle, with Portals for shot; and it is faced with stone Walls, where the Rock was not strong enough. The Houses have generally no upper Rooms; the Bazars are large. I saw here a fine Stone very much resembling Porphyry; being of a red ground, with yellow specks and veins, very glossy. It is dug just by *Antab*.

Antab is doubtless *Antiochia penes Taurum*: in the Skirts of which it stands, and is not far distant from the highest ridge: it is about two thirds as big as *Aleppo*.

Wednesday, April 26.

We passed through a Fruitful Mountainous Country, and came in seven hours and a quarter to *Rowant* Castle. It stands on the top of a round steep Hill, and has been strong for the times it was built in. It is probably a Saracen Fabrick, and is now in Ruins. At the foot of the Hill Westward runs the River *Ephreen*; its Course is South South West. Our Course from *Antab* to *Rowant* was North West and by North.

Thursday, April 27.

We continued travelling through the Mountains, which were now somewhat more uneven and precipititious,

titious, but watered every where with fine Springs and Rivulets. In about ſix hours we came to *Corus*; our Courſe was South Weſt, having croſſed the *Ephreen* about two thirds of an hour before. Juſt by *Corus* is the River *Sabon*, that is, *Chor* or *Char*, which encompaſſes moſt part of the City.

Corus ſtands on a Hill, conſiſting of the City and Caſtle. The City ſtands Northerly; and from its North end aſcending, you come at laſt to a higher Hill to the Southward, on which ſtands the Caſtle. The whole is now in Ruins, which ſeems to have been very large, walled very ſtrongly with huge ſquare Stones. Within are obſervable the Ruins, Pillars, &c. of many Noble Buildings. On the Weſt ſide there is a ſquare Encloſure of great Capacity, compaſſed with good Walls and five Gates, which admitted into it; as one may diſcern by the Ruins of them. I conjectured they might be the Cathedral. Over the Caſtle Gate was written the three Inſcriptions in the Plate belonging to page 7.

The middle Inſcription was over the middle of the Portal; the other two on the top of the Pilaſters on the right and left hand.

Below the Caſtle Hill, to the Southward, ſtands a noble old Monument. It is ſix ſquare, and opens at ſix Windows above; and is covered with a Pyramidical Cupola. In each Angle within is a Pillar of the Corinthian Order, of one ſtone; and there is a fine Architrave all round juſt under the Cupola, having had heads of Oxen carved on it; and it ends a-top with a large Capital of the Corinthian Order; near this ſeveral Sepulchral Altars, of which only one has a legible Inſcription, which you may ſee in the Plate.

Friday, April 28.

We left *Corus*, and without the Town about half a mile South Eaſt, we deſcended down through a way cut obliquely on the ſide of a Precipice, which leads to a Bridge of ſeven Arches of a very old Structure, over the River

River *Sabon*. And about a quarter of a mile further, we came to another Bridge of three very large Arches over the River *Ephreen*. These Bridges are very ancient, and well built of square stone. Three Pillars have an Acute Angle on the side against the Stream, and a round Buttress on the other side, and on both sides are Niches for Statues. They were well paved a-top with large Stones, and are doubtless, as well as that of the other side of the Town, the Work of the Excellent and Magnificent *Theodorit*.

From this Bridge in about three hours, with a Course South South East or South East and by South, we arrived at *Jan-Bolads*. From *Jan-Bolads* to *Chillis* is one hour and two thirds, Course North North East. *Chillis* is a large populous Town, and has fifteen Mosques that may be counted without the Town: and it has large Bazars. Many Medals are found here, which seem to argue it to be ancient; but under what Name I know not.

Aleppo bears from *Jan-Bolads* South and by East; *Seck-Berukel* South South West. An hour from *Jan-Bolads* is *Azass*. And two hours further, we lodged in the Plain, which about *Chillis* and *Azass* is very wide, and no less fruitful. This Country is always given to the *Validea* or Grand-Signior's Mother.

Saturday, April 29.

We arrived by God's Blessing safe in *Aleppo*, having travelled about five hours with a Course South and by East.

Δόξα Θεῷ.

OF

Of the VALLEY OF SALT, *Which is about Four Hours from* ALEPPO.

THIS Valley is of two or three Hours Extent; we were three quarters of an Hour in crossing one Corner of it. It is of an exact Level, and appears at a distance like a Lake of Water. There is a kind of a dry Crust of Salt all over the top of it; which sounds, when the Horses go upon it, like frozen Snow, when it is walk'd upon. There are three or four small Rivulets empty themselves into this Place, and wash it all over, about Autumn, or when the Rains fall.

In the heat of the Summer the Water is dryed off, and when the Sun has scorched the ground, there is found remaining the Crust of Salt aforesaid; which they gather and separate into several Heaps, according to the degrees of fineness; Some being exquisitely White, Others alloy'd with Dirt.

It being soft in some places, our Horses hoofs struck in deep: And there I found in one part a soft brown Clay, in another a very Black one, which to the Taste was very Salt, tho' deep in the Earth. Along on one Side of the Valley, *viz.* that towards *Gibul,* there is a small Precipice about two Men's lengths, occasion'd by the continual taking away the Salt; and in this you may ſee how the Veins of it lye. I broke a piece of it, of which that part that was expoſed to the Rain, Sun and Air, tho' it had the ſparks and particles of Salt, yet it had perfectly loſt its Savour, as in St. *Matthew*, Chap. 5. The Inner part, which was connected to the Rock, retained its Savour, as I found by proof.

In ſeveral places of the Valley, we found that the thin cruſt of Salt upon the ſurface, bulged up, as if ſome Inſect working under it had raiſed it; and taking off the part, we found under it Efloreſcences of pure Salt ſhot out according to its proper figure.

At the Neighbouring Village *Gibul*, is kept the Magazines of Salt, where you find great Mountains (as I may ſay.) of that Mineral, ready for Sale. The Valley is farm'd of the Grand Signior at 1200 Dollars *per Annum*.

FINIS.

THE INDEX.

A

ABel his Tomb pag. 134
Absolam his Pillar 103
Adam, the Earth He is suppos'd to be made off 128
Ager Damascenus ibid.
Alcoran carried in State ibid.
Alms House at Shoggle 5
—— and Mosque at Jebilee 13
Annanias his House 129
Annas his House 99
———— Tomb 133
Antidote of the Turks against Melancholy 129
Antonine Way 36. 38
Aqueduct conveying the Water from Solomon's Pools to Jerusalem 90
Aqueducts several at Bambych 154
Arms and Instruments of War anciently made use of 156
Author, His Beasts press'd for Publick Service 25
——In Danger of being Shot by a drunken Janizary 133
——In Great Distress by Bad Weather 8
——Entertain'd by the English Consul at Tripoli 25. 141
——Entertain'd by the French Merchants at Sidon 44. 118
——Entertain'd by the Guardian at Damascus 124
——Joyns the French Consul at Acra 56. 117
——His Letter giving some Account of the Turks 146
——His Letter concerning Gehazi's Distemper, and of Excommunication among the Greeks 150
——He leaves Jerusalem in Company with the Mosolem 110
——His Servants frighted away by those of the Bassa at Tripoli 32
——He sets out to the River Euphrates, &c. 153

B

Balls of Stone us'd for Ammunition 54
Balbeck Temple 136
Bashalick of Aleppo ends, and Tripoli begins 5
———— of Tripoli and Sidon 35
Bathsheba's Pool 101
Bay of Junia 35
Beautiful Gate of the Temple at Jerusalem 101
Bells an Abomination to the Turks 27
——Two at the Church at Canobine and at no other Place 143
Bell-Mount a Convent of Greeks 27
Bethesda the Pool of 107
Bird and Coney Islands 31
Bitumen a Kind of Earth resembling Pitch 84

Boats

Boats for Crossing the Rivers, the Fashion of them, and Manner of rowing them 156
Bridges, two near Corus, the Work of Theodorit 160

C

Cajaphas his House 99
Cain, where slain by his Brother 131
Caphar, a Duty paid by Travellers 4. 6. 17. 35. 43. 53. 58. 62. 67.79. 83. 111. 119. 121. 138.
Castle of Antab 158
——— of Beer 156
——— of Corus 159
——— of Merchab 17
——— of Margath ibid.
——— Several in the Bay of Junia, built by the Empress Helena 35
——— of Rowant 158
——— of Scandalium or Alexander 53
——— of Temseida 33
Cave, where the Apostles hid themselves when they forsook their Master 102
Cedars of Libanus 142
Cedron the Brook 102. 105
Ceremonies observ'd by the Latins on Good Fryday 67. 72
Chain cut in Stone 126
Chappel of the Holy Manger 91
Christ, the Place where he was Betrayed, Mocked, and Scourged 106, 107
——— His Prison 73. 99
——— Place of his Crucifixion, The Hole where his Cross stood, and the Cleft in the Rock made by the Earthquake 73
——— where he appeared to the Three Marys 98
——— Place of his Ascension 104
——— Transfiguration 113
——— where he fed the Multitude 116
——— where he was Smote by a Servant of the High Priest 99
Christian Church at Bellulca 7
——— ——— at Jebilee 15
Churches, their East End left entire 49
——— Chappels and Convents 98, 99
——— Convents, Palace, Nunnery &c. ruin'd at Acra or Acca 55
——— at Beroot 41
——— and Convents at Sydonaiia, 16 in Number 131
Church of the Cœnaculum 100
——— of Helena 98
——— of St. John at Damascus, and the Turks Tradition concerning it 125
——— and Convent of St. John, where our Saviour was Baptized 81. 93
——— at Sebasta over the Place where St. John was Beheaded 59
——— at Beer, in Memory of the Blessed Virgin 64
——— and Convent of Latins at Jerusalem 67
——— at Nizib 157
——— of the Holy Sepulcher 67. 94
——— at Tortosa 19
Clouds so low as to obscure the Road 142
Coffee House a Remarkable One near Damascus 128
Compliment made to the Consul by the Priest 28
Consul (French) at Sidon, visits Jerusalem every Easter 45
Convent of St. Anne 108
——— Over the Place of the Annunciation 112
——— Dedicated to Elias 87

——— Of

——Of Greeks, call'd Bell-Mount 27
——Of Greeks, called the Holy Cross 94
——Oozier 35
——Sydonaiia 130
Corn, the Eastern Manner of Gathering it in Harvest 144
Court, 55 Yards Square, cut in the natural Rock 20
Crutches us'd by the Priests at Divine Service 28

D

Damascus, its pleasant Situation, &c. 124
—— The Gardens, and the Manner of visiting them 130
—— Water'd by the River Barrady 122
David's Well 90
——The Place where He slew Goliah 92
Dead Sea 80. 83
——The Quality of it's Water 84
Desart, where our Saviour was Tempted by the Devil 79
Dike, a large one, cut in the Rock 30 Yards over, and more than a Furlong long, near the Serpent Fountain 20
Dolourous Way 107
Doors of Stone very remarkable 77

E

Elias his Stone Bed 87
Elizabeth the Mother of St. John, her House 93
EmirChibly encamp'd upon the Road, robs Travellers 58. 111
Eunuch of Æthiopia, where Baptized by Philip 92

F

Faccardine, Prince of the Druses, his Palace 39
——His Reason for turning Day into Night 43
—— His Grove ibid.
Figures of Men, carved in the natural Rock 37
Fissure, a very Deep One in the Earth 5
Font, us'd by the Apostles 98
Fountain of the Apostles 79
——Ayn il Hadede 140
——Ayn il Hawra 134
——Ambus Lee 119
——Of Elisha 80
——Of Kishon 115
——Of Selee 58
——Of the Blessed Virgin 53. 102
Fruit call'd Za-cho-ne remarkable for it's Healing Quality 86

G

Garden Walls at Damascus, described 124
Gate of the Temple wall'd up by the Turks, and why 103
Gethsemane 105
George (St.) and the Dragon, the Place where they Duell'd 38
Goads of Oxen, of an extraordinary size 110
Good-Fryday, how observ'd by the Latins at Jerusalem 67
Granite, several Pillars of it 15, 16. 31. 42, 43. 112.
Grott of the Blessed Virgin, an Account of the Whiteness of it 91
Grottos two Hundred, cut in the side of a Rock 118
——All Transactions related in the Gospels, said to be done in Grottos 114

H

Hadgees, the Manner of their setting out on their Pilgrimage to Mecca 127

Hermon, the Dew of it 57
Herod's Gate at Jerusalem 78
Holy Fire, a Ceremony on Easter Eve 94
——The Peoples great Opinion of it 96, 97
——Land begins 45
——Sepulcher profaned 108
Horse falls through the Bridge at Casimeer 48

I

Jacob's Well 62
——His Bethel 64
James (St.) where Beheaded 98
Idol Canis 36
Jebilee, it's Situation 13
——Anciently convenient for Shipping 15
——Remains of a Noble Theater there ibid.
Jehosaphat, the Turks Tradition concerning a Pillar there 103
Jeremiah the Prophet's Place of Residence, and Bed 76
——The Dungeon where he was kept by Zedekiah 78
Jerusalem, Ceremonies at entring the City 66
——The Circuit of it Measured 109
——The several Ceremonies observ'd there on Good Friday, and Easter Day, relating to our Saviour's Crucifixion 72, 73 &c.
Impaling, the Manner of that Punishment 141
Inns, none to be found on the Roads in Turky 2
Inscription to the Memory of the Emperour Antoninus 37
——On the Fountain at Balbeck 139
——Over a Gate at Beroot 42
——Over the Castle Gate at Corus 159
——On two Pillars of Granite, lying cross the Road 47
Joachim and Anna Parents of the Blessed Virgin, their House 117
John Baptist (St.) his Cave 92
——Beheaded at Sebasta 59
——His Head kept in a Church at Damascus 126
Joseph Sold by his Brethren at Dothaim 116
——His Sepulcher 62
——The Ground given him by his Father Jacob 63
Joseph (St.) his House where Our Saviour liv'd 113
——His Chappel 87
Judas, the Place where He Hanged Himself 102
——the Place where He Betrayed his Master 106

K

Kanes, Lodging Places for Travellers 2
——One cut into a Rock at Beer 157
Kishon, the Brook 57. 115

L

Lake Limone 139
——Or Sea of Rooge 3
Lazarus, his Castle and Sepulcher 79
Locusts 61. 92

M

Mandrakes 61
Manuscript of the Testament in Syriack 800 years old 98
Marine, near Tripoli 31
Mark (St.) his House 98

Marks of the Crofs &c. on the Arms of Pilgrims, the Manner of making them 75
Maronites, exacting and infolent 35
MaryMagdalen, her Habitation 79
——— the Houfe where fhe wafhed our Saviour's Feet 108
Mary the Virgin, where Born 108
——Her Annunciation 112
——Her Affumption 105
——A Story of Her Girdle ibid.
——The Place where fhe was warned of her Death 104
——The Place where fhe Dyed 100
——The Place where fhe Saluted Elizabeth 93
——Her Corpfe arrefted by a Jew 100
——Her Sepulcher 106
Miracle, related of a Picture of the Virgin Mary 131
Monument, at Corus 159
Mofques, fifteen at Chillis 160
Mount of the Beatitudes 115
———Calvery 68
———Carmel 54
———Gerizim and Hebal 59
———Gihon 108
———Moriah 68. 100. 106
———Olivet 79. 105
———Saron 53
———Sion 101
———Tabor and Hermon 57. 113. 115
Mountains of Caftravan and Climax 35
————Of the Franks 88
————Of Libanus, and Anti-Libanus 119. 139, 140
————Of Occaby 6
————Of Offence 102
————Of Precipitation 116
————Of Quarantania, from whence the Devil fhewed Our Saviour the Kingdoms of the World 80
————Where the Swine ran down into the Sea 115
————Of Arabia 80
————Of Gilboah 115
————Of Gilead 66
————Of Paleftine 65

N

Neceres, a ftrange and fingular People 12
Nehemiah, his Well 102
Nicephorus (St.) a Story concerning his Beard 41
Nox Tenebrofa, Good Fryday fo called by the Latins at Jerufalem 72
Nunns, disfigure their Faces, to avoid the Beaftialities of the Souldiers 55

O

Orange Garden at Beroot 40

P

Paffengers impos'd upon by thofe who Affift them at the Rivers 44
Paul (St) the Place of his Vifion, &c. And where He was let down in a Basket 129
————The Houfe where He lodged at Damafcus 133
Peter (St) his Prifon 98
————The Place where He Wept, after denying His Lord 100
Pidgeons, great Numbers of them at Kefteen 3
————One put into the Cupola of the Holy Sepulcher, to reprefent the Holy Ghoft 96
Pilate, his Palace 106
Pilgrims, at Eafter guarded from Jerufalem to Jordan 78
————Difturbed

——Disturbed in their Devotions there 83
——Their Feet wash'd by the Father Guardian 94
Pillar of Lot's Wife 85
Plain of Acra 53. 117
——Of Esdraelon 57. 111. 115
——Of Galilee 115
——Of Jericho 66. 80
——Of Junia 24
——Of Tripoli 142
——Of Zabulon 117
Potters Field 101
Presents, to be sent when you intend a Visit to the Turks 26
Princes Bridge, suppos'd to be Built by Godfrey of Bulloign 26
Promontory, suppos'd to be mention'd by Strabo 32
Promontory (White) 52
Pulpit, of Tortoise Shell and Mother of Pearl 99

Q

Quails 61

R

Rachel's Tomb 87
River Abana and Pharpar, suppos'd to be Barrady 121
——Of Aleppo arises from a Fountain 158
——Awle, near Sidon 44
——Ayn Yentloe 121
——Barrady 121. 134
——Belus 56
——Beroot 38
——Casimeer 24. 48. 120
——The Cold Waters 24
——Damer or Tamyras 43
——Eleutherus 24. 48. 120
——Ephreen 158
——Euphrates 155
——Ibrahim Bassa, suppos'd to be the River Adonis, it's Water of a Bloody Colour at certain Seasons 34
——Jobar 16
——Jordan 81
——Kishon 57
——Letane 119, 120
——Lycus or Canis 35
——Nahor Abrosh, or Lepers River 24
——Nahor Acchar ibid.
——Nahor Hussine 18
——Nahor Kelp 36
——Nahor il Kibber, or the Great River 24
——Nahor il Melech, or the King's River 16
——Orontes, it's Water and Fish unwholsome 4
——Sabon, Chor or Char 159
——Sejour 154. 158
——Towzad 155
Rivulets, the Manner of Cleansing them at Damascus 124
Road cut on the side of the White Promontory 52

S

Sand, a Material for making Glass 56, 57
Sea of Tiberias 115
Seditions sown by the Turks among the Wild People 56
Sepulchres hewn into the Rock 14
——Of the Kings 76
——The Doors of them very surprizing 77
——Of the Prophets 104
——Of the Virgin Mary, St. Anna and St. Joseph 103
——with six Statues and Inscriptions 132
Sepulchral Monuments, very Large 21
Serpent Fountain 20. 24
Sheck's House, a Burying-Place 9
——Wife, a Deep Fissure in the Earth 6

Shepherds,

Shepherds, the Field where they watch'd their Flocks, when they received Tidings of the Birth of Christ 90
Siloam, the Pool of 102
Simeon, his House 87
Sion Gate at Jerusalem 99
Sion, the Hill of 69
Solomon's Cisterns 50
——— Fountains, Pools, Gardens &c. 88
——— High Places Built 102
——— His Strange Wives kept at Siloe ibid.
Spon (Mr) drown'd in passing the River Damer 43
Star appeared to the Eastern Kings 87
St. Stephen, the Stone on which He suffered Martyrdom 103
——— His Gate at Jerusalem 78. 103
Stones like Pease, a Tradition concerning them 87
———Resembling Porphyry 158
———Sixty one Yards long, in a Wall at Balbeck 138
———Of a sulphureous Nature and Combustible 84
———Three much Esteem'd, and why 99
Stone which was laid at the Door of our Saviour's Sepulcher 99
Stone of Unction 74. 97
Stone said to have the Impression of our Saviour's Feet upon it 103, 104
Stream issuing out of the side of a Mountain 119
Street called Straight, at Damascus 133
Synagogue, where our Saviour Preached 113
Sultan Ibrahim, His Tomb, Mosque, Grotto, Cell &c. 13, 14

T

Theater, the Remains of a Noble One at Jebilee 15
Thomas (St.) his House 98
Tomb and Cell of Sultan Ibrahim 13
———Several, in the Plain near Latichea 11
Tortosa, anciently Orthosia, a Place of Great Strength 18
———a Large Castle there ibid.
Towers, or Sepulchral Monuments 21
Tree, from whence our Saviour's Cross was taken 94
Tree (Olive) to which our Saviour was Chain'd 99
Tribe of Asher 45
———Of Zabulon 57
——— Of Benjamin 64
———Of Manasses and Ephraim 58
Tripoli suppos'd to have been Three distinct Cities 31
Troglodytæ, a People mentioned by Strabo 118
Turks Byram or Ramadam, a Feast after Lent 108
———Their Manner of Building, and Furnishing their Houses at Damascus 125
———None of them live above Two Years in Boote-shellah 91
———Their Tradition concerning a Pillar at Jehosaphat 103
———Their Story of their Prophet viewing Damascus 121
———Their Policy in sowing Divisions among the Wild People 56
Turpentine Tree, under which the Virgin Mary reposed Herself 87

V

Valley, where the Angel destroyed the Army of Senacherib 91

——— Of

——Of Be-da-me 5
——Of Bocat or Bicath-Aven 119
——Of Canobine 143
——Of Elah 92
——Of Hinnom 101
——Of Jehoſaphat 78. 102. 104
——Of Rephaim 87
——Of Salt 161
——Of Sychem 59
Vaults, ſeveral very Large at Jeruſalem 100
——Twelve, in Memory of the Apoſtles 104
Viſit, the Manner of it in Turkey 29

W

Wilderneſs and Convent of St. John 91, 92
Water and Fiſh in the River Orontes, very Unwholſome 4

Z

Zaccheus, his Houſe 81
Zachary, his Sepulcher 102
Zebedee, his Houſe 98

CITIES, TOWNS and VILLAGES, Mentioned in the Journey.

ACamy 153
Achzib 53
Acra 53. 117
Adjia 157
Antab 158
Arab 58
Arvad and Arphad 19
Ayta 120
Azaſs 160
Bab 153
Balbeck 120. 134
Bambych 153
Baneas 17
Barſeba 59
Be-da-me 5
Beer 64. 156
Bell-maez 4
Bellulca 7
Berook 44
Beroot or Berytus 38
Beſack 18
Bethany 79
Bethlehem 87
Bethulia 115
Bezay 153
Bird and Coney Iſlands 31
Bocat or Bicath-Aven 119
Bootеſhellah 91
Botrus and Byblus 33
Callemone 32
Cana of Galilee 117
Canobine 142
Caphar-Milki 119
Carmel 43
Caſtravan ibid.
Caypha 57
Chillis 160
Citte-Galle 7
Cinga 64
Corus 159
Daberah 115
Damaſcus 119. 122
Demas 121
Dioceſaria 117
Dothaim 116
Dyr il Daab 153
Eden 119. 142
Endor 115
Engedi 88
Eſſoyn 2
Geeb 64
Gibul in the Valley of Salt 162
Gibyle 33
Hadyar ib Sultane, or Sultan's Stone 6
Harbanooſe 3

Howar

Howar 63
Hozano 2
Jan-Bolads 160
Jebilee 12
Jeneen 111
Jib Jeneen 120
Jerabolus 155
Jericho 81
Jerusalem 66. 86
Jordan 81
Julia Felix 38
Keffre 2
Kefteen ibid.
Kor Aren 120
Ko-ri-e 48
Latichea 11
Leban or Lebonah 63
Lediff 153
Legene 2
Legune 57
Maday 134
Meneen 131
Merakia 18
Meshgarah 119
Mesopotamia 157
Michmas 64
Modon 92
Nain 115
Naplosa 59
Nazareth 57. 112
Nizib 157
Oo-rem 2
Orthosia 18
Patrone 33
Philip (St.) 92
Ptolemais 54
Rama 58. 66
Rooge 3
Roselayn 50
Ruad, supposed to be Arvad and Arphad 19
Samaria 58
Saphet 115
Sarphan or Sarepta 48
Satyra 117
Sawee 63
Sebasta 58
Seck-Berukel 160
Selwid 64
Sepharia 117
Sherack 59
Shoggle 4
Sholfatia 8
Shuckfoat 43
Sidon 44. 117
Silam 157
Siloe 102
Sinie 133
Solhees 122
Sophia 18
Sodom 85
Sultan's Stone 6
Surbass 153
Surgawich 134
Sychem or Sychar 59
Tall 131
Tekoah 88
Te-ne-ree 4
Tortosa 18
Tripoli 25. 141
Tyre 48
Uwur 157
Uzzi 120
Ye-ad 139
Zib 53

FINIS.